THE VISION AND THE VOICES OF
IEDC-BLED SCHOOL OF MANAGEMENT
25 YEAR LEARNING HISTORY

Publishing of this book was made possible by the kind support of Studio Moderna and its President Mr. Sandi Češko.

IEDC–Bled School of Management
Prešernova cesta 33
4260 Bled, Slovenia www.iedc.si

CIP - Kataložni zapis o publikaciji
Narodna in univerzitetna knjižnica, Ljubljana

378.6:005(497.4Bled)(091)

MIRVIS, Philip H.
The vision and the voices of IEDC - Bled School of Management : 25 years learning history / Philip H. Mirvis and Danica Purg ... [et al.]. - Bled : IEDC - Poslovna šola, 2011

(978-961-6720-15-1)

257808640

THE VISION AND THE VOICES OF IEDC-BLED SCHOOL OF MANAGEMENT

25 YEAR LEARNING HISTORY

Philip H. Mirvis

and

Danica Purg

Arnold Walravens

Nenad Filipović

Nadya Zhexembayeva

Melita Rant

Ian Sutherland

→ CONTENTS

INTRODUCTION

→ THE END OF HISTORY OR BEGINNING OF THE FUTURE?

"All management books, including those I have written, focus on managing other people. But you cannot manage other people unless you manage yourself first." These were the opening remarks of a lecture by Peter Drucker, world-renowned management sage, then 86 years old, beamed by satellite from his home in Claremont, California to a conference hall in Ljubljana, Slovenia, in October, 1996.

The occasion? The 10th anniversary of the founding of the International Executive Development Center (IEDC), a Slovene business school whose animating mission circa 1986 was to prepare a new generation of Slovenian and Yugoslavian managers to lead enterprises toward a market economy. The school was then based in an estate in nearby Brdo which had been Josip Broz Tito's summer residence as President of the Socialist Federal Republic of Yugoslavia from 1953 till his death in 1980. In the Socialist era, it operated as a training center for "leading workers in the economy"—managers chosen by workers' councils in their companies and other organizations.

Those in attendance for the anniversary conference included hundreds of managers from Slovenia and neighboring countries, newly unleashed business owners, top government officials, participants from the school's "short courses" during its first ten years and graduates from its Executive MBA program, launched in 1991, as well as IEDC faculty, staff, participants, supporters, and a smattering of journalists and dignitaries.

Drucker, born in Vienna in 1909, was reared in the "old Europe" traditions of the Austro-Hungarian Empire, which included Slovenia, and he carried onward a commitment to personal ethics, social civility, and civic-mindedness to his studies of law and employment in an export company in Germany, then to private banking in England, and later to international journalism and university teaching in the United States. Throughout his life he railed against the class-ridden bureaucracy of European states and businesses, spoke out early and forcefully about the specter of Nazism, and criticized Socialists for embracing fanatical nationalism prior to World War I and for enfeebling enterprise and initiative following World War II. His lineage and outspoken ideas made Drucker a kindred spirit among the IEDC assemblage but it was his perspective on management that they had come to hear: at that time, there was no word for "management" in the Slovene vocabulary.

Many in the audience had been through a liberating and tortuous past 10 years. The period encompassed the breakup of Yugoslavia and fall of the Berlin Wall; "shock therapy" via the introduction of market capitalism and closure of state-run factories and farms and firms run by workers' councils; and the invasion of Slovenia by the Yugoslav army when it declared its independence in 1991, horrific fighting and mass slaughter in Bosnia and Croatia among Muslims, Croats, and Serbs from 1992 to 1995, and then NATO's military intervention in the region.

On the global tableau, the end of the cold war and fall of the Soviet Union, and closer to this story, the collapse of Yugoslavia and independence of its member states all factored into what political scientist Francis Fukuyama called the "end of history." It is said, however, that the arts see and represent the new well before the sciences, and surely before it is expressed in politics and business. Thus artists and filmmakers in the region, chronicling the first steps of the rocky transition to democracy and openness in poetry and theater, put a different spin on Fukuyama's thesis: rather than the "end of history" the artists wondered, could it instead be "the beginning of the future"?

Backdrop to the Story

This biography of IEDC is a jointly-told tale based on interviews with key people, group discussions with faculty, staff, and business leaders about major events over the school's 25 years, as well as scholarly reports and media commentary about the school. The study concerns leadership, starting with IEDC's President and Dean Danica Purg who overcame resistance from communist party apparatchiks in founding the school and from Western accreditation bodies in placing it prominently on the world stage. It also focuses on managing and what it takes to build a world- class institution in a region rich in intellect and academic tradition but ravaged by economic hardship and ethnic wars. Finally, it provides a glimpse of modern history—witnessing the transition from socialism to capitalism, from an inward- looking to market-facing economy and, in the classroom, from dry academic lecturing and recitation to interactive case study and project-based learning.

The primary setting is Slovenia (a country roughly the size of Massachusetts in the U.S.) set amidst the Alps, which borders Italy to the west, Croatia to the south and east, Hungary to the northeast, and Austria directly north and has a small portion of coastline along the Adriatic Sea. It was settled originally by Illyrian and Celtic peoples and was part of the Roman Empire in the first century B.C. It became a more or less Slavic country in the 6th century A.D. when settlers migrated from the east (the Ukraine today) and also settled in Serbia and the Balkan mountain nations to the south. Flashing forward to the 1500s, Slovenia accepted Austro-Hungarian rule to protect itself from Turks occupying South Eastern Europe and, like Croatia, was primarily Roman Catholic.

Following the defeat and collapse of Austro-Hungary in World War I, Slovenia declared briefly its independence then joined with Montenegro, Serbia, and Croatia in 1918 to form a new nation called the Kingdom of the Serbs, Croats, and Slovenes. The name was later changed to Yugoslavia ("South Slavs") in 1929. During World War II, Germany occupied Yugoslavia and Slovenia was divided among Germany, Italy, and Hungary. Slovenes fought a guerrilla war against the Nazis under the leadership of the Croatian-born Communist resistance leader called Tito. In 1943, Slovenia joined with Bosnia and Herzegovina, Croatia, Macedonia, Montenegro, and Serbia to form the Socialist Federal Republic of Yugoslavia under Tito's leadership. Aligned with the Eastern bloc during the war and in the aftermath, Yugoslavia adopted a position of geopolitical neutrality after the Stalin-Tito split in 1948.

After Tito died in 1980, Serbian leaders in Belgrade sought to concentrate political and economic power. In defiance, Slovenia's leaders set out on a path of reform and began their press toward independence. It is against this backdrop that IEDC transformed from the "Center for Educating Leading Workers in Economy" into an international management school.

Part I Synopsis: 25 Years of Making History

Part I of this volume contains the 25 year learning history of IEDC with chapters covering the founding of the school and its growth to adolescence by taking "the best from the west" and tailoring it to the Central and Eastern European (CEE) context; how it expanded its reach throughout CEE countries and into the heart of war-torn Bosnia; and how it innovated in its teaching methods and content to be acclaimed in 2002 by British Minister for Europe Peter Hain as "the best small business school in Europe" and to be recognized in 2010 in the Aspen Institute's global rankings as one of the most innovative schools in the world. The chapters unfold in roughly chronological order with some backtracking and detours to put the school's development into historic, regional, or thematic perspective.

Best from the West

In the first chapter, we meet Marko Bulc, Director of the Slovene Chamber of Commerce, which operated the school for leading workers. Its curriculum—chiefly lectures on economic and political developments in the region and presentations by state and chamber officials—was no longer suited to the rapidly changing environment in the region. Explaining his intent in changing the direction of the school, Bulc offered this nuanced proposition, "A socialist country can have a market economy," mindful that the communist party would be watching his every step.

When asked whether or not Slovenia was then ready to compete in the market, Bulc replied, "The gap is not in technology, but in the minds of people." He invited Professor Danica Purg, a Slovene teaching in the Faculty of Organization of Work, to prepare the new concept and curricula for the school. In 1986 she was appointed Director and set out on a whirlwind tour that took her to the leading management school - INSEAD, outside of Paris, and later to IMD Lausanne, London Business School and Harvard Business School--to learn more about modern management education and to invite professors to her school in Brdo. These visits opened her eyes to possibilities but added a modifier to the school's mantra: "take the best from the west *and leave the rest*."

Meanwhile, she encountered strong resistance to proposed changes in Brdo's profile and curriculum. Coming the first day to her new office, she found this message scribbled on a desk calendar by the former director of the school: "This cow will destroy our school."

Her first five years at Brdo were driven by pragmatism and featured short (one- to two-day) courses on the basics of business aimed at practicing managers. But the content was new and fresh for the practitioners who reported: "It was exciting. We didn't know anything about private ownership, competitive strategy, or accountability. And in English!" The school launched a seven-week General Management Program in 1987. "Not just training, but a development program," a proud graduate remarked. By 1990, participants from Romania and Hungary joined in and some 54 faculty members from abroad were engaged in lectures, short- courses, and programs tailored to Slovene companies.

Still, Danica was restless: "I noticed during the early years at the school that students simply accepted lessons without question and with little reflection. It bothered me. I wanted to make things more interesting for them and, particularly in a country that was going through political change, I wanted to prepare leaders for a better world that requires deeper thinking and questioning. I believed we needed to develop not only leadership skills, but also more critical thinking and creativity."

Chapter 2 chronicles how Western professors partnered with IEDC faculty member Nenad Filipović to introduce more interactive instruction and establish student learning team projects in local businesses; IEDC also launched an Executive MBA. The transition wasn't easy reports René Magdalenić, from a management development consultancy in Belgium: "The managers in class weren't used to working in teams. They were very individualistic, hierarchy-minded, and secretive. It was difficult to provoke contradictory debate."

Over time, however, a more fluid teaching-learning environment took shape and according to René, open discussion and disagreement "became a rule rather than the exception." Another visiting faculty member, Nancy Adler from McGill in Montreal, reports, "I remember one conversation with a group of IEDC executive participants about socialism versus free markets. It was the most reasoned conversation I have ever been a part of—stripped of all the ideology and described through the lived experience of people who were winners and profoundly understood the strengths and weaknesses of both systems."

From Taking to Sharing

With the breakup of Yugoslavia and breakdown of the Iron Curtain, Western Europe and the U.S. rushed financial resources, advice, and assistance to CEE countries to advance business education. Management savant Tom Peters came to lecture about "the American way of managing" and the European Foundation for Management Development (EFMD) invited Danica to become its first board member from the CEE region. Still, as one insider put it, "Cocky American and Western European professors marched in to teach and didn't know a damn thing about Eastern Europe."

Fed up with being patronized by Westerners, and fired up by the notion that management development in their region would accelerate if CEE business schools charted their own course, Danica joined with 12 other deans and Derek Abell to form the Central and Eastern European Management Association (CEEMAN). Its headquarters would reside at IEDC which was moving into a new phase of its development in the mid-1990s–from taking the best from west to sharing know- how and experiences with peer institutions and leading businesses.

Chapter 3 develops this theme of co-learning in the context of Slovenia's 10 day war over independence and subsequent fighting between Serbs, Croats, and Bosnians in the Balkans. It follows a group of European executives in the aftermath to bomb-blasted Sarajevo where, guided by Danica and U. K. Professor Jonathan Gosling, they met with Prime Minister Zlatko Lagumdžija, film-maker Haris Pašović, and other political and business Bosnian leaders to reflect together on tragedy and transformation.

In early 2000, IEDC moved from Brdo to two manor houses repurposed for management education in the alpine town of Bled, Slovenia. An MBA student, Shahin Lauritzen, described his arrival at the campus: "Here, I thought, at the foot of the Julian Alps, in the tranquility and the crispness of the Slovene mountains, and Bled Lake, where the Slovene knight Črtomir fought so heroically for his beliefs, was truly a unique opportunity to find focus and indulge in the study of business administration and leadership."

At this time, IEDC also published the Slovene-English Dictionary of Business Terms: manager translates as vodja or direktor.

Leading through Innovation

Danica reports in chapter 4 that "Art can be a tool for leadership development....it helps you become more creative, innovative and inspired. It promotes reflection." A troupe of internationally recognized musicians such as Miha Pogačnik (Slovenian violinist), Marko Letonja (Slovenian conductor), Peter Hanke (Danish conductor), and Paul Robertson (British violinist), plus various vocal and instrumental ensembles, film-makers, and visual artists began to enrich the leadership development experience of IEDC participants. They led workshops on deep listening, music and teamwork, embodied forms of leadership, and creativity in music and management.

This marks a third transition in IEDC's development: it is now truly innovating and exercising thought leadership in management education.

U.S. and to some extent European business schools were from 2001 onward swollen with MBA students being prepared for "number-crunching" jobs in investment banks, consulting firms, or big businesses undergoing regular restructuring and resizing. IEDC participants learned their numbers, too, but they were also being readied to operate in the emerging "creative economy," where design and aesthetics are sources of differentiation for business, and in an "experience economy," where customers are engaged by and actively participate in the production of goods and services. Here, again, the arts seem to see new things before they appear in business practice.

Chapter 5 shows IEDC continuing to innovate as its pedagogy and students' attentions turn to the "green economy" and to expanded visions of corporate social responsibility (CSR). On its 20th anniversary, the school promoted "leadership for a better world." Thereafter it adopted Principles of Responsible Management Education, advanced by the United Nation's Global Compact, and led the Global Compact chapter for Slovenian businesses. In summer, 2011, IEDC hosted a conference to build a European network for CSR with the participation of the Clinton Global Initiative. And its faculty coordinated a research project to identify and promote "Hidden Champions" among mid-size businesses and with CEEMAN ran a worldwide contest, "Challenge:Future," that enlisted students to develop innovations to make a better world.

As IEDC moved forward on these fronts it attracted a who's who of management scholars--John Stopford, Jean-Pierre Lehmann, Bill Fischer, Pedro Nueno, Hermann Simon, Edgar Schein, Nancy Adler, Manfred Kets de Vries, and Ichak Adizes among them—to visit and engage with program participants. As of this writing, IEDC has hosted over 55,000 participants from 70 countries; led programs for more than 300 companies worldwide; and created a faculty network of 100 plus professors from the world's leading business schools.

teleconference, arranging for two satellite linkages in case one failed. Danica left Claremont on "cloud nine" having accomplished, in the words of a colleague, "whatever she sets her mind to." She never got the snapshot; "too embarrassed to ask," she confides, but there is a signed photo of Peter Drucker in her office, offering warmest wishes, and a file of correspondence beginning in 1995 up until his death in 2005.

Now that mythic story has elements of the epic, comic, and romantic; it also offers some pragmatic lessons about the importance of networking, personal influence, and persistence in leading an organization and says something about Danica as a leader. As she reports, "I visited Drucker two years later and I liked the compliment that he gave me that he had 'never met a bigger entrepreneur than me.'" She then adds, "He called me 'Donika' and I never corrected him."

Part II starts off with an essay by Danica on leading and networking. Contributions include:

- "Networking and connecting are important for leaders," says IEDC founder Danica Purg. What does it take to successfully network? Among the personal characteristics needed she lists "openness for the new and change, energy and enterprise spirit, passion and persistence, excellent communications skills, and full commitment to work." Her essay includes examples of these attributes in building the school. On this count, note that an article in the *Financial Times Deutschland* headlined Danica as "Madam Energy."

- Peter Drucker writes that management deals with "actions and application," making it a technology, but then adds that "management also deals with people, their values, their growth and development—and this makes it a humanity." Accordingly, managers should draw on the insights of both the social sciences and humanities, of economics as well as history, of physical science and ethics, and so on. In this spirit, Arnold

Walravens, faculty of IEDC, reviews the themes– about business and society, as well as the art and science of management, developed in top lectures and forums at IEDC over its 25 years.

- Warren Bennis and James O'Toole, in an article in the *Harvard Business Review* on "How Business Schools Lost their Way," contend that the schools today suffer from "an overemphasis on rigor and an underemphasis on relevance. Business schools have forgotten that they are a professional school." Nenad Filipović, Academic Director of IEDC, makes it his job to ensure that his colleagues never forget that IEDC is a professional school. His stance: "outward looking, understanding the market and educational needs, keeping in touch with reality." He describes his school's work with management development programs for organizations and with project-based learning for students.

- Speaking at IEDC's 10th anniversary, Drucker's message on personal development was this: "Find out what you are really good at and then make sure you place yourself where your strengths can produce results." IEDC faculty member Nadya Zhexembayeva, born in what was then the Soviet Republic of Kazakhstan, is a devotee of positive psychology, a strength-based approach to human development, that is for her about "awareness, awakening, consciousness." She emphasizes learning through questions, rather than answers. On a typical class day, her executive MBAs will spend some time in small dialogue groups practicing "appreciative inquiry"–reflecting on peak experiences in their personal lives, on success moments in business and civic life, and on what's going right in their worlds. Her job is to enhance the "quality of the questions" and to stimulate more "transformational thinking" about how to build on past achievements when tackling current personal and organizational challenges.

- Melita Rant, a Slovene who grew up in an area devastated in World War II, also had to learn a lot about management when she joined IEDC. Trained as an economist, she had no familiarity with social psychology, sociology, or the "soft stuff" when she joined the school. Today, she has adapted the methodology developed by German Professor Hermann Simon to identify "hidden champions" in Slovenia—mid-size businesses, largely unrecognized by the public, that develop leadership in export market niches. She is leading a team of researchers from many CEE business schools to identify and profile champions throughout Central and Eastern Europe. The team has found that what distinguishes hidden champions is not only their technology, but also "out of the box thinking," and what Melita describes as the "extraordinary vision of the founder."
- Recently, the school hired Ian Sutherland, a Canadian pianist, management scholar, and budding maestro in the classroom, to further develop its curricula in arts-in-management. This is the "new, new thing" in management education. The business schools at Stanford and at Toronto have aligned with design schools. The intent is to re-introduce beauty and imagination into the management calculus and to stimulate creativity and wonder in management students. Why do Danica and Ian favor arts in management education? They write, "The creative processes which underlie novel and inspirational artistic products and experiences have much in common with leadership. Engagement with art has the capacity to stimulate novel thoughts and ideas, challenge our beliefs and assumptions, and connect us with the social and material worlds around us in profound ways."

Part II closes with a few personal reflections and highlights some questions raised from experiencing IEDC and its people, history, and environs.

IEDC – 25 YEARS MAKING HISTORY

→ FOUNDING YEARS

For the 10th anniversary celebration of IEDC at Brdo in 1996, Milan Kučan, head of the League of Communists of Slovenia in 1986, President of the Republic of Slovenia from 1991 onward, reflected on the school in this way: "We can, if we wish, look at the past, present, and future of IEDC in terms of numbers which tell of us its beginnings, its development, and its possibilities. But no matter how telling the numbers are, they cannot tell us everything. In particular, they do not show the crucial role IEDC played in drawing the attention of the business community and the general public to the necessity of high quality education for executives in Slovene companies... Nor do they tell of the people who stand behind the ideas of high quality, professionalism, and excellence in this creative work... I congratulate the Director of the Center, Dr. Danica Purg and her colleagues on their achievements over the past ten years."

Today, 15 years later, his full head of hair grayer, his face more lined, Kučan harkens back to Danica's decision to take up leadership of the Chamber school. "I was surprised," he says, turning to Danica, "I thought you'd be in politics, maybe my old job," he smiles. Or in the arts or university or something else—perhaps an international public figure and reformist like her countryman Slavoj Žižek?

Danica was 39, with flaming reddish hair, artsy interests, and full of élan when she became Director of IEDC. Her biography could have taken her in many different directions. She had been to Paris for the student protests in 1968 and active in Yugoslav politics ever since; she had a passion for theater, especially Shakespearian drama; she'd earned her doctorate in political science from the University of Belgrade; and she had become a voice for worker's interests in the nation and abroad, often appearing on radio, in print, and in the public eye.

As Kučan reflects back to IEDC's founding years, he credits Marko Bulc, head of the Chamber of Commerce, for courage in challenging the Slovenian communist party to "open our eyes" and to "understand Western ways." "The idea of private business was new to us," he says, "In the former Yugoslavia everything was considered social property." And while Kučan embraced the need to re-orient the economy to Western markets, what surprised him was that "I had to change my own mentality, too."

There were, according to Kučan, several actors behind-the-scenes that countered resistance and mobilized support for the makeover of the Chamber school. President of Slovenia, Janez Stanovnik, economist and fellow WWII partisan with Tito, swayed Kučan and influenced the party to "not oppose" a new direction for the school. Dr. Peter Kraljič, head of McKinsey & Co.'s consulting practice in Germany, returned to his native Slovenia like a Prodigal Son to promote the idea among the business community. Derek Abell, then outgoing Dean of IMEDE Lausanne and a prominent professor, helped Danica to recruit top flight Western faculty and gave the made-over school a "credible academic aura."

"So you see," Kučan continues, "the school has many fathers," but, he adds, "only one mother."

Leadership as Autobiography

In his studies of political, business, and cultural leaders, Howard Gardner contends that "leadership is autobiographical" and that leaders influence others through "the traits they embody." These traits are not inherited, Gardner notes, but are developed through the life course, the highs and especially the lows of the leader's journey. Another leadership scholar, Noel Tichy, contends that life experiences ultimately shape a "teachable-point-of-view" about leadership that extends from the actions and stories of the individual leader to the leadership culture of his or her organization, and to the broader society. In this spirit, consider some bits of Danica's coming of age as a leader.

"Determined, passionate, persistent, courageous, a fighter" are how her friends and colleagues describe Danica Purg. They also say "pushy" and "stubborn" and like "hell-on-wheels" when it comes to enlisting faculty, shaping curricula, and demanding the best for her students and school. Danica acknowledges these traits, some more to her liking than others, and recalls two incidents in her formative years that illustrate them.

She and her classmates, six years old, had been promised a grammar school field trip to Maribor, a cultural center some 40 km away from her village. The trip was cancelled—"I don't remember why, only that it didn't seem fair"—so she collected five of her friends and instead of going to school headed to the train station, fished out Yugoslav dinars from her pocketbook to pay the fare, ultimately got off at the wrong station, walked another hour into Maribor where she had a fine day's visit, including seeing her surprised aunt who gave her some money, white coffee, and a slice of her special bread. She was scolded on return, but not "too severe," and, laughing, grants that it was a "teachable moment" in her early leadership development.

In the other instance, when she was 10, a classmate was being "picked on" by a teacher, and Danica again rounded up some friends to visit the principal of another school in a village close by and air their complaints. They marched to the principal's apartment building, climbed the stairs, and met her on the roof where she was hanging up laundry to dry. The principal heard them out, challenged their interpretations of events at points, but ultimately took the matter to the town assembly and the teacher was reprimanded. This time Danica was praised, rather than scolded, for acting on her convictions.

Danica was born February 2, 1946 and grew up in a poor region of eastern Slovenia. Her father, a blacksmith, worked in machine maintenance in a factory, and was a leading voice in the local worker's council. Her mother, a textile worker and later a housewife, and two sisters complete the family configuration. Danica was the eldest child, a factor in her take-charge personality so friends say; her two younger sisters were respectively "clever" and "interested in cultural matters," but not so inclined toward academia or leadership.

Danica's father, however, was very much an enterprising leader and doer, and an early role model. He helped to bring electricity and running water to the local village. The family got one pig, then another, then a cow, motorbike, and a radio which "opened me up to the big world out there." Mother taught different lessons: She encouraged Danica to visit a new girlfriend in a Serbian town where 7,000 men, women, and children had been killed by the Nazis in WWII. That memory would be invoked later in Danica's life when she took business executives to see and learn from war torn Sarajevo.

Finishing high school she, like many of her compatriots, followed Tito's advice, "If you learn your country you will love it even more." At 18, she was a brigade commander for a cadre of international students—Danes, East Germans, Serbs, and so on—building roads in Montenegro. Her uniform was a borrowed blouse with badge labeled Polska that became her nickname in the crew. During weekends she learned to drive, touring country roads in a beat up Fiat. She sent a note to her mother asking for funds to apply for a driver's license. Her mother replied, on an old bread wrapper, "You're working, let them pay for it." This was another step for Danica toward self-sufficiency.

At 19, Danica entered the University of Ljubljana, beginning the scholarly, artistic, political, and international forays that 20 years later would catch the attentions of Bulc and Kučan. One experience that foreshadowed her future sensitivities and leadership agenda occurred at the Sorbonne, in Paris, where she studied French while working for her living. She felt a "little bit strange" in the city and certainly at the Sorbonne where many of the students were more worldly and wealthy. In her telling, she had three things going against her: "I was a woman, a socialist, and a peasant from Yugoslavia."

Her self-picture and confidence were restored, however, in an assignment to re-imagine Voltaire's enigmatic novel *Candide* in the contemporary world. While the original story is a satirical critique of optimism, it ends with the admonition that "we must cultivate our garden." Some of the literati see this as advice to retreat from society. Others contend that it advances the philosophy that the world (the "true" garden) can be improved not with idle optimism, but instead by hard work and industry.

The teacher singled out two student papers for praise. One, by a Latin American, was a Marxist critique of supposed progress in his nation. The other, by a Slovene, told of a gritty little girl "working her way through the system," and succeeding. It was full of "poetical metaphor," Danica recalls, adding, "I was always proud to be from a worker's family."

Yugoslavian Self-Management

Danica remembers fondly her first meeting with Tito. In high school, she was chosen as a top student to visit Tito in Belgrade for his birthday. She danced with him and in all the cinemas throughout Yugoslavia her dance with Tito played on newsreels the next day.

Born Josip Broz, the nation's president became known as Tito when he took over leadership of the Communist party in Yugoslavia in 1937. One legend is that it was his nomme de guerre, chosen because the owl "tito alba" is a creature of the night. Another traces it to the Roman general Titus. A humorous version is that he earned the nickname by telling subordinates where to go and what to do—You (*ti*) will do this (*to*) or You (*ti*) will do that (*to*). Famously authoritarian, the Croat-Slovene was much loved by most of his countrymen for leading partisans against the Nazis in WWII and for resisting Stalinism and gaining his country's independence from the Soviet orbit.

Fearing a Soviet invasion in the late 1940s, Tito relocated industry from Yugoslavia's western border in Serbia to Croatia and Slovenia. He also helped to develop the concept of Yugoslav "self-management" that, on a macro scale, led to economic decentralization and liberalization. On a micro scale, it gave workers a democratic voice in the goals, operations, and daily work in their organizations and had them elect their managers. All of this was regarded as socialism operating from the "bottom-up" as compared to the Soviet "top-down" model.

The Yugoslav Federal Assembly passed laws in the early 1950s to implement the self- management scheme. These laws replaced state with so called "social" ownership of the means of production and empowered enterprise workers' councils to set production plans and take the most important decisions. Company directors were chosen by workers' councils. The government also reformed economic planning and freed some prices to fluctuate according to supply and demand, but kept control over foreign trade. Private ownership was limited to agriculture, services, transport, crafts, and tourism, amounting to only a small portion of the overall economy. The communist party separated itself from the state but remained a monopoly political force.

This system seemed to serve the multi-country nation well. From 1952 to 1965, Yugoslavia's economy grew an average 4.46 percent annually. Living conditions, health care, education, and cultural life improved, religious freedom flourished, travel restrictions were abolished after 1960, and artists moved away from socialist realism and into abstract-symbolism and other experimental forms. The Yugoslavian model was variously eyed with envy and trepidation in parts of Central and Eastern Europe making up the Soviet bloc. It was a factor in the Hungarian uprising of 1956 and the Czechoslovak movement known as "Socialism with a human face" in the spring of 1968.

Furthermore, the self-management model in industry gained international notice. It embodied industrial democracy and seemed to be a powerful antidote to alienation and bossism in the workplace. A workers' council decides whom to hire, what wages to pay, and how to allocate profits remaining after taxes and operating costs. Unlike a trade union, which negotiates with management via collective bargaining, a workers' council, in theory at least, more or less runs the organization.

This idea had strong appeal among a progressive set in Western Europe and especially the United States where social movements supporting blacks and women were achieving gains and calls for work reform were being heard in reports about the "blue collar blues" in factories and "white collar woes" in offices. Senator Ted Kennedy held congressional hearings on worker alienation in 1972 and signs of discontent—rampant absenteeism, shoddy workmanship, growing numbers of grievances, and lower productivity—were documented in a national report on the declining state of *Work in America*. Meanwhile, higher quality Japanese cars and electronics began entering the market and appealing to consumers.

Scholars around the world examined possible solutions for the malaise. They studied new models for organizing production, such as Volvo's approach to team assembly and Japan's quality circles. They also explored new ways of running an enterprise— including worker cooperatives in the Basque region of Mondragon, the Israeli kibbutzim, and the Yugoslav system of self-management. It was at an academic conference on industrial democracy in 1972 that one such scholar, Danica Purg, based in Belgrade, met another one, Arnold Walravens, a lean figure with curly hair and laughing, lively eyes from the Netherlands.

Arnold and Danica: A Scholarly Romance

As Arnold says, it's a nice story about how he and Danica met and "quite romantic." Prior to attending a lecture at the conference on industrial democracy, he met an old friend who had been traveling in Afghanistan, became sick and had gone, according to Arnold, "a little bit crazy." The two old friends had some drinks and together sauntered into the lecture boozy and loud. Finally, a red-haired conferee, supervising the proceedings, came up and charmed him by saying, "If you are quiet now, we will have a coffee together later."

That evening Arnold listened to Danica's critique of comparative research on the satisfaction of workers in Yugoslavia, the U.S., Italy, and Israel. She argued that the study which found workers in the U.S. more satisfied with their jobs than those in Israel and Yugoslavia textile industries was misleading. It was an "old-fashioned, positivistic study, just numbers," Danica railed, "No attention to context." "When supervisors are elected," she went on, "and workers set their own targets, everyone feels a greater sense of responsibility." "Aspirations, meaning, learning," Danica explained, are what are important to consider in judging a workplace. Arnold readily agreed; their coffee was prolonged by a dance, and romance was in the offing.

Through their courtship, and after marriage, Danica and Arnold lived sometimes together and sometimes apart, each pursuing their own careers. Arnold continued to work as a professor at the Delft University of Technology in the Netherlands and to pursue his interests in arts as a "Sunday painter." Danica returned to work in the government in Belgrade where she was also a postgraduate student. In 1976, after spending four years in the "Federation," she returned to Slovenia and began to lecture at the university on the theory and practice of self-management.

In classes, she would speak of the many benefits of self-management but also reminded her students that factories in Yugoslavia operated along the same scientific management principles as those in the west–work was divided into simple, repetitive tasks and paced by the mechanization of the assembly line. To illustrate the dehumanization of this "chain gang" work, she had students watch Charlie Chaplin's *Modern Times* and compare it to team-oriented production systems. She took her students on field trips to local factories where they could talk to workers and "understand what they are thinking and feeling." And she created with them a series of television documentaries which won a national prize.

In addition, she read poetry to her classes and showed students photos of the massive wall murals by Mexican artists Diego Rivera, José Orozco, and David Siqueiros that illustrated vividly the oppression of factory work. One that she showed them, Rivera's 27-panel *Detroit Industry* frescoes, finished in 1933, had outraged Henry Ford whose massive River Rouge auto assembly plant was just downriver from the museum housing the mural. Mr. Ford had wanted it destroyed, just as Rockefeller had done when Rivera painted a mural featuring protesting workers (including Lenin leading a May Day Parade) for his Rockefeller Center in New York City. In this case, however, Mrs. Ford intervened and Rivera's Detroit mural remains on view today.

Was Danica propagandizing her students? "Not at all," she counters, this was a "system for organizing work everywhere in the world–no matter communist, socialist, or capitalist." All of this gained her a following among students on the campus, and more broadly, as she also did periodic talks on the radio and gave magazine interviews. It also earned her the enmity of some professors who favored the traditional model of giving a lecture, or "reading" as it was called, and whose syllabi hewed to more scholarly literature.

Did Self-Management Fail?

There is considerable debate over whether or not the Yugoslav experiment in self-management was a failure. What is incontrovertible is that the region's economy and society declined dramatically from the late 1970s to 1985. Industrial productivity fell 20 percent, worker's incomes dropped 25 percent, and education, health, and housing services were unable to keep up with public demand. By 1986, inflation had skyrocketed to 150 percent per annum. What is more, the income gap between Yugoslav republics widened, to the point that Slovenes earned more than twice that of their countrymen from Macedonia and Kosovo.

Certainly macroeconomic factors contributed to Yugoslavia's steep descent from its "golden age" of two decades prior. The state was heavily in debt having borrowed, as a nonaligned nation, from both the East and West to fund the growth in social services. It owed the International Monetary Fund (IMF) nearly $20 billion USD in 1981. Geopolitics was a factor, too. Russia was not inclined to reach deeper into its own shrinking pockets to fund the breakaway "South Slav" experiment with socialism. And the Reagan administration pressed for repayment of American loans. Recently declassified documents reveal that this was part of a strategy to promote "a 'quiet revolution' to overthrow Communist governments and parties" (U.S. policy also foresaw reintegrating the countries of Eastern Europe into a market-oriented economy).

Finally, some of the blame has to focus on the state's centralized planning for foreign trade and the overall economy. On this point, former Yugoslav economic minister Svetozar Vukmanović-Tempo once famously said that the best strategic weapon that his nation could use against the U. S. would be to send over two Yugoslav planners to help ruin the American economy!

Did the system of self-management also fail? Critiques note that Yugoslavia's system, while a mix of socialism and capitalism, limited most private business ownership and thwarted initiative. Unprofitable firms could not be sold-off; it was difficult to start new businesses; and, in any case, an emphasis on equality in economic relations made entrepreneurship suspect. Finally, faced with rising inflation in the early 1980s, workers' councils raised wages and unemployment rose further.

Do Something for Your Country

Danica and Arnold, while firm believers in the principles of worker self-management, also saw deeper problems in the Yugoslav context. "Workers (including leading ones) didn't know anything about economics, accounting, marketing," Danica noted, and "nothing really about managing work systems or even people." Arnold added, that although people were smart and could take care of themselves in Yugoslavia, they "only thought they knew something about private business, maybe from watching television shows (like Dallas), but not too much about how markets work."

Marko Bulc and other leaders of the Slovene Chamber of Commerce were of course aware of the decline in Yugoslavia's economy overall and in Slovenia, too. Still, they saw that their nation also had many advantages versus the others in the region. For example, although Slovenia comprised only one-eighth of Yugoslavia's total population, it was the most productive of the region's republics by far, accounting for one-fifth of total Yugoslav GDP. In addition, it was far more market oriented and Western-facing, contributing 30 percent to the Yugoslav export in 1985.

To support his case for reform, Bulc referenced studies by Slovenian Professor Aleksander Bajt on how socialist economies incorporate market pricing mechanisms. Bajt, a Ph.D. mentor to U.S. President Bill Clinton's economic adviser Laura D'Andrea Tyson, was an internationally recognized expert in economics and his views carried weight in Yugoslavian academic and political circles. As Bulc described it, "It was clear to some of us that there was only one way for the Slovenian and the Yugoslav economy: opening up and being included in the world. The slogan at the time was 'export to convertible markets.' Courage alone was not enough. What was essential was the knowledge of the conditions in these markets, since otherwise it would have been impossible to adapt, not to mention be better and competitive."

Slovenian companies had some joint ventures with the West at that time, but most business people's knowledge was limited to operating in a small market, with socialist "mutual relationships." One facet of the Chamber's reform plan was to expand business people's knowledge of international markets through a series of visits to companies and universities in the United States. (Interestingly U.S. business leaders went off to Japan at this time to study total quality management.)

More dramatic was the idea to create a new school at the Chamber–a school to develop managers. This was not an easy sell. "Everybody who dared to put forward a strong and decisive vision of introducing professional management was seen as a technocrat," Bulc recalled. "The market of labor, goods and capital was not recognized; the economy was dominated by self-management. However, there were more of us who were convinced that even in socialism it is impossible to be successful without considering market rules."

Describing his thinking about the Chamber school, Bulc knew that the old director would have to go and the new one would need to be "young, liberal, and energetic." He had met Danica, knew of her innovative teaching and administrative reputation, and believed she was the best candidate. Bulc offered Danica the position and promised her his full backing along with that of other Chamber Board members.

Danica recalls consulting with friends, confidants, and Arnold who challenged her: "If you ever want to do something for your country, this is it!" She signed up for the job in fall, 1985, after she and Arnold had visited a seminar on management in Helsinki, organized by Henley college, where she met the first colleagues (among them a Japanese professor) who would later come to lecture to her school. This was, she reports, her first participation in any management seminar because until then, "I was dealing only with self-management."

A Tricky Leadership Transition

In the best of circumstances, leadership transitions have to be managed carefully (they are likened to "passing of the baton" in a relay race); in more complex cases, they require a delicate combination of planning, improvisation, cunning, and determination. Danica's leadership transition would be very tricky.

First, it foreshadowed the reinvention of the Chamber school, encompassing its mission (what we do), operations (how we do it), clientele (for whom), and personnel (by whom). Bulc and the Chamber had laid out the purpose (why we do it) and agreed upon a general direction for the new school, but they had not developed the rest of the story. To begin to flesh this out, Danica interviewed the presidents of over 50 leading Slovenian businesses to detail the new concept for the school and define its curriculum. She also analyzed the programs at two executive education centers in Europe (Ashridge in the U.K. and INSEAD in France). This was packaged into a voluminous document addressing the "what, how, who, and why" for reinventing the school.

Second, the transition would bring an "outsider" into the organization. The 100-plus faculty members who lectured part-time at the Chamber school at that time were based in political organizations throughout Yugoslavia and in various universities. Many of the school's part-time faculty knew Danica for being "straight-forward" and "courageous in tackling change," but some of her university colleagues, especially those from the Faculty of Organization of Work who also taught at the Chamber school, were opposed to Bulc's choice (perhaps for those very reasons).

Finally, and critically, the school's then current director and some staff were strongly resistant. It would take some time and maneuvering to ease them out of the picture. Bulc and Danica agreed therefore to phase her into the post by preparing two short seminars based on the new concept for the 50 presidents of companies that Danica had interviewed.

To diminish the tension among faculty and staff, Bulc called a meeting to bring a select subset of 15 of them together to discuss the proposed program. On the day of the meeting, as he and Danica were preparing their presentations, a secretary rushed in and informed them that the school's entire faculty insisted on coming to the session. As Danica tells it, "we were for a moment wondering what to do and then decided to go on." Bulc phoned the President of the Council of the Chamber school, Dr. Lev Premru (then Chairman of Lek, an important Slovene pharmaceutical company) to enlist his presence and support.

Bulc introduced the prototype program to full assemblage but once the faculty got the chance to react to it, they disparaged it by saying that there was nothing useful in the curriculum; that the concept was a copy of the Western schools; that it did not fit with the Yugoslav self-management system; and that it was not scientific, properly pedagogical, and so on. Danica was taken aback by the tone of the criticism and what seemed to be an orchestrated attack on the whole concept of creating a management school. She wondered how Bulc would handle things. He kept his cool by hearing everyone out and then thanking them for their support adding that their remarks were useful and would be surely taken into account. It was, according to one observer, "salto mortale" (a daring and dangerous jump with possibly lethal results) that Bulc had executed "masterfully." Another described it as "masterful manipulation." In any case, it was now understood that change was coming and that Danica would be taking charge.

Naturally, resistance did not end with the meeting. Rumors circulated that Danica's "foreign husband" could be a spy. And wouldn't the Western professors bring in imperialism? Rather than address every rumor and resistor, Danica and Bulc worked out the program on corporate governance that would be launched for the 50 company presidents.

At the first of these programs, a well-known professor had prepared a four-hour introductory lecture on corporate governance which served as a basis for the new legislation in Slovenia. However, the lecture was didactic in the "old-style" and Danica noticed that the audience was fidgeting and tuning out. She interrupted and called for a break. Bulc objected that the break was not necessary. Nevertheless, Danica insisted on the break and during it told the professor to shorten his remarks and take some questions.

Next day, during a debriefing, Bulc chided her for acting like a military sergeant barking orders to the troops. She replied, with something of a smile, that she had behaved more like a general—taking charge of the situation. "That earned his respect," Danica recalled. It also gave her the freedom to build the new school in her own way. She reports:

> On Monday, February 2, 1986, on my birthday, I entered the estate Brdo (the former residence of late president Tito) and identified myself at the main entrance. Some minutes later I walked into hotel Kokra, where Center had its facilities. The day was cold and the eight employees of the Center received me coldly too, because they did not know what to expect. The director's office was closed (he took a sick leave!) and I had to go to the reception of the hotel to get the key. I cleaned the table (where there were his personal belongings, like gloves and the calendar with the message "this cow will destroy the school") and I started to work. This was my first day in the beautiful 25-year long story of building up the IEDC-Bled School of Management.

The Best from the West

While the school at Brdo offered short courses in its first year of operations, interest was growing for something with more depth and from a leadership perspective. While Arnold continued to teach in Holland, he also found himself in an unusual position for an academic: a member of the Supervisory Board of the Dutch publishing company Wolters Samson, now known as Wolters Kluwer. He came to the post via his studies of worker self-management in the Netherlands: it seems he had met with the company's Employee Works Council; they liked what he had to say; and they nominated him as one of their representatives to the Supervisory Board. With this new connection, he talked with Danica and they agreed to "do something together."

Soon the entire executive team of Wolters was at Brdo in a seminar with 40 or so Slovenian CEO's. "It wasn't like a professor lecturing," Arnold recalls, "They were exchanging information with colleagues." The Wolters Samson Board shared their frameworks for competitive analysis, market segmentation, and positioning. All of this talk about competition was shocking to some of the Slovenes, Arnold recalls. Why so? "They didn't like to talk about competition so publicly."

There was also spirited discussion of the two-tiered governance model used in Holland where an Executive Board made up of company managers runs day-to-day operations and a Supervisory Board of non-executive directors, representing stakeholders, oversees the Executive Board. It was interesting to the Slovenes that workers had a voice in firm governance, but they wondered whether the Supervisory Board could take an independent position.

In 1987, the school launched its first longer program, a seven week General Management Program (GMP). Hellmut Schütte, a Professor at INSEAD, who studied economics and business in his native Germany and earned his doctorate from the University of St. Gallen, Switzerland, came to Brdo to teach marketing and strategy. Jean-Pierre Lehmann, a Frenchman with a doctorate from Oxford, dialogued about globalization and international management. And René Magdalenić later joined the team for finance. All of the coursework was in English.

Jean-Pierre would grab the participants' attention immediately with remarks like this: "Somebody once said that the problem with communism is communism, whereas the problem with capitalism is capitalists." This would segue into a discussion not only of the business manager's moral compass but also about the responsibilities of business in an emerging market. He would caution the managers about "diploma disease" and the idea that a degree means you are educated as a manager. He would later pen his views: "Education has a much broader and deeper meaning; it is not confined to time or space, it is an attitude, a constant search for learning founded on an insatiable curiosity. An 'educated' person is not only someone who knows a great deal, but someone who wishes to learn in any circumstance, who poses questions, who probes, reflects and assimilates, to gain both knowledge and wisdom." In saying so, he was very much echoing Danica's wishes for her new school and program participants.

René, meanwhile, was teaching finance for nonfinancial managers--"the content of this program was in this part of Europe completely new, because the bookkeeping system and everything else under self-management was different." He explains that the participants "are not interested in the mathematics of it or in academic discussions of what is 'theoretically right' or 'wrong.' Their main interest and intellectual effort goes to 'what is useful' or 'not useful' to support their decision making. Our answer to that is to work with a lot of everyday practice-oriented case studies and exercises."

In addition, he adds via email, "more than a half of the participants were women executives, which you must admit, is for us a new experience (lol). In Holland we have now and then some female participants during a financial seminar, but it never exceeds one or two percent...."

In the next few years, the school would organize international conferences on technological change, doing business in China, doing business in the Soviet Union, and the like and host seminars with visiting delegations from as far away as Zambia and as nearby as Kosovo. In 1988, for the launch of its President's Forum, the School issued its first of what would become an annual lecture or Book of the Year, "Ways to Industrial Success," by McKinsey's Peter Kraljič who was then an IEDC board member.

The Chamber, in turn, led delegations of Slovene young managers, with support from the U.S. State Department, to New York, where they met business leaders and professors from Columbia, and to Cleveland, Ohio. There the delegation would meet a budding business manager on his own quest of discovery.

Janez Škrabec, Quest of Discovery

One of the early friends of IEDC, and later one of the co-owners, was Janez Škrabec, a Slovene who founded Riko, a company involved in industrial engineering, logistics, and construction. Janez was a free spirit in his school days, travelling to the U.S. In 1986, at age 18. He purchased a Greyhound bus ticket, for $300 USD, to "see the country." On the east coast, he concentrated on the U.S. political capital, Washington, D.C., and the commercial capital, New York City. By day, he would tour the Capitol building or Smithsonian museums in DC, talk with tourists, locals, and politicos, and then take the overnight bus to NYC, sleeping on board to save money on lodging. Next day he would visit Wall Street or climb to the top of the Empire State Building, then travel on the overnight train back to DC and begin again.

The U.S. west coast was the real treat. Hollywood was "exciting," but Janez was more turned on by Silicon Valley where he saw high technology industries buoyed by venture capital taking shape. He met Apple co-founders Steve Jobs ("didn't like him") and Steve Wozniak ("really liked him") and found his own entrepreneurial imagination sparked. On the bus, he read *Lee Iacocca: An Autobiography*. Lessons on taking to market the iconic Ford Mustang and turning around the failing Chrysler Corporation also stayed with him.

In the U.S. heartland, stretching from Oklahoma to Ohio, Janez found the soul of the country. He recalls meeting a pious Jehovah's Witness hanging clothes to dry in her backyard. "Imagine her shock when I told her about Marxism and such," he chuckles. But he marveled at the freedoms. He also grimaced at the poverty he observed, and read John Steinbeck's *Grapes of Wrath*, on the hardships facing farmers during the depression of the 1930s, to get a deeper feel for "contradictions of capitalism" in the U.S. This too shaped his thinking and led him to the conviction that he would be a different kind of businessman.

Janez completed his travels with a visit to Cleveland State University, where he took classes and met a group from the Slovene Chamber of Commerce doing their own study tour of U.S. businesses and management education. There he learned about the "new" chamber school and about Danica Purg.

Returning to Slovenia, he would study economics at the University of Ljubljana and later participate in several programs at IEDC. In 1991, he would build the Riko Group. A blurb about the business gives a flavor to its roots and culture: "Riko originates from the Ribnica valley, which is located a mere 50 km to the south-east of Ljubljana. More than 500 years ago, the inhabitants of this place began manufacturing and selling wooden household products all over the Austro- Hungarian Empire and even beyond its borders. For many centuries, this business-- combining entrepreneurial spirit, craftsmanship, commercial ambitions, and marketing approaches--provided a good life for the inhabitants of the Ribnica valley and developed and refined their values in the course of the centuries, equipping them with iron discipline, diligence, flexibility, and innovativeness."

Under Janez, Riko further developed its heritage of wood crafting into the building of wooden houses. Cooperation with distinguished investors and designers, including Philippe Starck, with whom a new line of prefabricated houses is being developed, has strengthened Riko's position on the West European market. Entrepreneurship, professionalism, and flexibility of Riko's engineering approach have also helped the company in strengthening its position on the Eastern markets. Riko reconstructed the Hotel Peter I in the Moscow Centre, built automated warehouses, including IKEA's distribution centre in Moscow, and has become a strategic partner to Russian automotive giants such as Autodizel and Autovaz.

Reflecting on what makes his company work, Janez says, "We have developed consensus among generations: you will find all ages in our team, from students to pensioners. We are more successful because we balance between youthful enthusiasm and bravery on the one hand, and calm wisdom on the other. My father, for instance, is 78 years old and retired, but he is still an active member of the company. And this also holds true for others who have retired, but still work with us." Why? "Because Riko's culture is entrepreneurial: sooner or later you will get captivated by the spirit of entrepreneurship which does not die when you retire. Everybody at Riko asks how to do even more for the company."

Lessons on Leading

As for his lessons from IEDC, Janez recalls the emphasis on leadership in the curricula. Today he sees the distinction between leadership and management in this way: "The leader has to show the target to be fired on, the manager must, in the right way, make sure the target is a good hit." He also recalled a very personal takeaway: "I learned something interesting from Professor Kets de Vries. He said that the most successful people and companies are those that are most worried. A Japanese professor made a similar statement. He said that the most successful companies are paranoiac. I find this really reassuring because there was a time when I worried so much about everything that I considered taking therapy. Now I understand that worrying is not all that bad."

Janez and his company are today active supporters of the arts, heritage, and social causes. "My personal system of values developed as early as my teenage years, and solidarity with humanity has become a basic value of mine. Today I look at this solidarity as an important heritage of the previous system," he explains. Additionally, "when my entrepreneurial skills were being honed through my experiences, I realized that investing in the growth and development of the environments where I am active is a necessity...." Reflecting this view, he recently took a Slovenian choir to Russia, met again Russian leader Vladimir Putin ("an important relationship for business"), and became president of the Slovene-Russian Business Council.

Janez, tall, lean, smartly dressed, a winning smile, is also a high profile Slovenian business leader. He is frequently covered in the business press and has been interviewed by *Playboy.SI* about his doings. "If you have a good reputation, you must also appear in the media," he says. "Those who are at the forefront of business... must understand their role and become important public figures and thus affect the fact that they also see and understand others as leaders."

What is the message Janez gives to IEDC participants with whom he meets regularly? "I know from experience that I am quite interested in the world of business and culture in terms of geography, history, and also character because I am a Slovene--and I highlight my specific traits at appropriate moments. I always find specific characteristics--on a personal or national level--interesting; there is an attractive aspect in every one. We should not forget that near and far are equally important, that we are whole and effective only when we have and cherish both wings and roots."

Prof. Danica Purg with Mr. Marko Bulc, president of the Chamber of Commerce at the opening of IEDC, 1986

Yugoslav Prime Minister Dr. Ante Marković, Deputy Prime Minister Mr. Živko Pregl, Prime Minister Mr. Dušan Šinigoj and President of Republic of Slovenia Mr. Janez Stanovnik visiting IEDC, 1986

Prof. Derek Abell, former dean of IMD Lausanne, lecturing at IEDC, 1989

First MBA Class with Prof. Jim Ellert and the participant from Ukraine Dmitry Chernobay, 1991

MBA Class 1991

Marko Mayer, Hellmut Schütte and Danica Purg at IEDC conference, 1991

Zambian managers studying at IEDC, 1988

High Chinese delegation visiting IEDC

Minister of Finance Dr. Marko Kranjec, Prof. Danica Purg, Prof. Hellmut Schütte and Prof. Tom Peters, 1993

Prime Minister Dr. Janez Drnovšek, Prof. Derek Abell and Prof. Hellmut Schütte, 1991

Graduation General Management Program, 1991

Dr. Peter Kraljič, member of the Supervisory Board of IEDC, Prof. Danica Purg and President of Republic of Slovenia Mr. Milan Kučan, 1991

Designing Presidents' MBA with Prof. Jim Ellert, 1992

President Milan Kučan and Prof. Aleksander Bajt, member of IEDC Supervisory Board at the MBA graduation, 1993

President of Chamber of Commerce Mr. Joško Čuk and Mr. Horst Weitzmann, Chairman of BSW, Germany

Violinist Miha Pogačnik in the class on art and leadership, 1993

Ms. Jerca Mrzelova, singing after the international conference, 1993

Visiting Peter Drucker at his home in California 1996

Prof. Nenad Filipović in GMP Class, 1995

→ TAKE THE BEST FROM THE WEST—AND LEAVE THE REST

The first business school in the world, the Ecole Superieure de Commerce of Paris, was established in 1819 to respond to the need for more formal management training brought about by the Industrial Revolution. In 1884, the first Bachelor of Finance degrees were granted by the Wharton School of Business at the University of Pennsylvania in the U.S. The Tuck School of Business at Dartmouth College was formed in 1900 to grant a master's degree in commerce and the Harvard Business School in 1910 offered the first MBA. Today, over 160,000 MBAs are awarded annually in the U.S.—triple the number awarded in mid-1980s. The MBA degree is now offered in more than 100 countries and is a globalized credential.

The first business school in Central and Eastern Europe, The Handelsakademie Pest (now Budapest Business School), dates from 1857. As IEDC began to internationalize in 1990, however, there were no MBA degrees offered in CEE countries. Students with an interest in management would study law or economics or political science. Non-degree management development programs offered by schools or universities were rare. Today, by comparison, the Central and Eastern European Management Association (CEEMAN) lists 192 schools globally focusing on emerging economies.

Writing about management education in emerging markets, Professor Derek Abell distinguishes between resource-driven, cost-driven, and knowledge-driven economies. A resource economy needs knowledge in planning and technology; a cost economy requires operations management expertise; and a knowledge economy depends on innovation and marketing. It also needs managers who can lead people. This is where Danica and Derek positioned Slovenia and IEDC.

Prophetically, Derek argues that the "spread of knowledge in our field is top-down. It starts from the Anglo-Saxon part of the world and particularly from the U.S., and then it spreads out like a trickle-down cascade. I am convinced that it could go the other way. In other words, if we had this kind of knowledge and started teaching it, we might discover some real universal generics of leadership and management that have not originated in Boston. They can originate here or in any part of the world."

Derek Abell

Derek Abell, a tall, white haired, accomplished specialist in marketing and strategy, was born on Britain's Isle of Wight, started his professorial career at the Harvard Business School, and joined IMEDE (Institut pour l'Etude des Methodes de Direction de l'Entreprise) in Lausanne, Switzerland as its dean thereafter. A merger of this school with another in the late 1980s would put his career on a new trajectory. The merged school, called IMD (International Institute for Management Development), was built by compromises on both sides. The campus would be located in IMEDE's Lausanne. But the deanship would go to the head of the other school. As a result, Derek found himself at "loose ends."

Danica recalls meeting Derek at an AACSB (Association to Advance Collegiate Schools of Business) conference in Canada. On the flight over, she read about the two schools' upcoming merger, consulted the conference program, and noted he would be speaking on a panel where she hoped to meet him. IMEDE, originally funded by Nestlé, was a professional school for practicing managers, unconnected to a university, and in the top ranks. Thus it was a good match for benchmarking the best in management education.

They met coincidentally in an elevator at the conference hotel, and listened later to each other's lecture. Danica "chatted up" Derek about her school. "You must come to Slovenia," she insisted. Derek, recalling their first meeting, said, "I didn't even know where Slovenia was! But I was interested. I had a background in strategy and general management and had been a dean for nine years, and not to be conceited, told Danica that there are a lot of things here you don't understand." Two weeks later he was in Slovenia and, as he put it with good humor, in the "spider's web."

Danica then interjects: "May I say something. Derek is a builder. He likes to see the challenge. And he is really a builder," she laughs, "He comes to the school that is in construction with a meter and measures the space between the chairs in a classroom!"

Actually Derek had bigger things in mind. "I had been at MIT and was hired to bring computer technology to the Harvard Business School. But I was thinking this is not me, you know, this is not my real purpose in life. My real purpose in life has to be to help these people think more broadly about what they're doing." During his visit, he discovered that Danica also had "big ideas about ethics, aesthetics, and literature in management education." "She intuitively grasped the big picture," he recalled, "and suddenly I thought jeez, that's interesting, these people in her part of the world could do more with this than I had imagined. They are culturally developed; they have a broader view of the world."

"And so," he went on, "we were very complementary in this way. It was a good fit. It still is a good fit!" Derek approved of the curriculum's initial emphasis on marketing, accounting, and cost management. The next steps were to flesh out the program with more on finance and strategy and to advance Danica's larger vision, step-by-step, starting with ethics.

Launching an Executive MBA

James Ellert, a soft-spoken Canadian, studied for his MBA at Western Ontario University, took a Ph.D. at the University of Chicago, taught at Queen's University in Kingston Ontario, midway between Toronto and Montreal, and made his way to IMEDE Lausanne in 1981 to head the MBA program. A professor of finance and strategy, he was introduced to Danica by Derek Abell. The three of them joined arms to create an International Executive MBA program that was launched in 1991.

As Jim describes it, "we spent a full day, in a locked room, no windows, and thrashed out the design and beginnings of a curriculum." He then enumerated the key design features:

1. The education would be practical more than theoretical. "Real world, real learning" (an IMD slogan).

2. Students would participate in compulsory study groups. During the day and after class.

3. It would be a modular, multidisciplinary program. Virtual faculty.

4. A center-piece would be a consulting project.

5. A module would conclude with an integrative experience.

As for this integrative experience, students would receive a business case and prepare analysis for review by the faculty who would give it a "critical reading." The students would have one day to "fix" the case and then make their final presentation. An Executive MBA graduate at IEDC described the intent of the overall experience as "mindset reconstruction."

It was mindset reconstruction for the faculty as well. Jim remembers his first teaching at Brdo: "it was essentially a hotel; we had a rectangular classroom, long and narrow; it wasn't easy to move around or get close to students sitting in the back." Still, there were advantages: "no restaurants or bars on the campus or nearby; we had a captive audience." He likened it to a "boot camp" atmosphere,"with students often working till midnight."

It was also hard to get across key ideas in finance and strategy. "Students were unfamiliar with financial methods like income statements, balance sheets, the financial markets." Accordingly, time was devoted to covering the basics. In addition, the language and business terms were unfamiliar. "Sometimes we would have to wait for an English concept to be translated into German then Slovene and finally to other local languages." Nonetheless, he found that students "gradually got in the swing of it."

Business Case Teaching

As they did at their home institutions of IMD, INSEAD, LBS, Harvard, Western Ontario, and the University of Virginia's Darden School, the Western faculty imported to IEDC used the business case study methodology to teach MBAs and practicing managers. Briefly, the case method is described as instructor-guided, discussion-based learning. It introduces complex, often uncertain real-world scenarios into the classroom with the protagonist, typically a manager, faced with an important decision. As Harvard professor, Roland C. Christensen sums it: "The case method represents a shift from the traditional, instructor-centered model of education to a participant-centered one in which students play a lead role in their own and each other's learning." Faculty, in turn, "pursue opportunities and 'teachable moments' that emerge throughout the discussion, and deftly guide students toward discovery and learning on multiple levels."

This approach to teaching-and-learning was dismaying for IEDC management students in the early 1990s. "Many were reticent to get involved in the classroom," Jim recalled, where it was considered "rude" to challenge a professor. "They were more comfortable talking in groups." Initially, he adapted the pedagogy to let students discuss the case among peers before it was openly examined by the entire class. Today, "that's ancient history," he adds, the challenge instead is to get animated MBA students to "wait their turn" in the classroom, not least so that they can listen first to what others have to say.

When asked why he came to IEDC and returned so frequently, he first spoke to the motivations of some of his fellow faculty in the EMBA program: Jan Kubes is from the Czech Republic, Jean-Pierre Lehmann has socio-political interests, Tom Vollman, the operations guy, was interested in self-management, and so on. Was it all about personal interests and connections? Looking up, he shakes his head no and explains that many of his colleagues were deeply committed to producing better managers and took it as a personal mission to "help out" in the CEE region. As for his own motivations, he says simply that he likes to teach and loves students.

Then, of course, there was the "personal touch" of Danica, the "great networker." Jim recalled that in 1994 he was scheduled on a flight from Geneva to Zurich to join Danica and travel onward to Ljubljana. His flight to Zurich was delayed by rainstorms. Meanwhile, at the Zurich airport, Danica cajoled the pilot to wait nearly an hour before taking off, so that her faculty member could be with his students next morning. Jim arrived in Zurich, rushed from his in-bound flight to the out-bound one, walked up the aisle to his seat and, as he describes it, "met cold stares from the passengers but a warm smile from the dean."

Teaching Ethics

Instruction in business ethics was imperative in the school's curriculum. Arnold recalls that many of the managerial students from the newly independent Slovenia and its sister states equated the free market with a caricature of American-style capitalism: "No taxes, no regulation, no rules, just free, free, free." Some had developed "bad business habits" from the old regime, involving bribery, political favoritism, and corruption, and in the free market model determined "If it's not against law, what's the problem?" When Arnold began teaching corporate governance at IEDC, "I got hit with a few tomatoes." But through the combination of having students ponder Drucker's "mirror test" and lively case discussions of ethical dilemmas in management, "understandings gradually shifted.

Danica recalls that as she started to introduce ethics into the curriculum, she couldn't find a professor for this subject, and so invited a Slovene bishop to lead the module. His lecture went well until the Q&A session. A student asked, "What is more ethical: to lie to the government that you are in debt so that the state gives you monies to pay the salaries of your workers, or to not lie and have to dismiss some people?" The bishop replied, "I cannot answer. I never thought about these issues."

Then a team of managers from General Electric came to an IEDC program. The team visited nearby businesses to get a first-hand look at Yugoslav markets and management practices. There they met Croatian Nenad Filipović who talked intelligently about business and had a good sense of humor. They told Danica about him and said "you should hire him." Nenad's company was then rocked by a scandal, his boss committed suicide, and the entire management team was fired. So Danica wooed him to Brdo, and he began assembling case studies and exercises for an ethics course that got good reviews.

Student Teams and Projects

Nenad, now Academic Director of IEDC, angular jaw, always crisply clothed, a businessman turned academic, operates like Danica's alter-ego: Whereas her imagination can sometimes put her "head in the clouds," Nenad professes to keep his "feet firmly on the ground." And while she draws in ideas, faculty, and pedagogy from around the world, Nenad has put his attention to developing home grown management education experiences.

With the ethics course underway, Nenad then met Professor Jan Kubes from IMD, a former consulting partner in McKinsey & Co. At IMD, Jan was experimenting in the early 1990s with "project based learning" wherein student teams work as consultants to an organization–the teams use interviews and fact-finding to diagnose the sources of their client's problem, then dig deeper and often reframe the issues to be addressed, subsequently review their analysis and findings with a client, and finally prepare action recommendations. Jan brought this pedagogy to IEDC and Nenad took it and ran with it.

The lessons from project based learning come from two directions. First, students have to learn how to work as a disciplined team. Rok Šabjan, an MBA student from Slovenia, with a background in physics, acknowledges that it is a "challenge to survive in a team." Why so? "Everyone has the right answer. Who is leading: my peers or the facts? It is hard to convince the group." Then there is the matter of engaging the client and motivating action. You have to "stop, think, feel," says Rok. "Management tasks and responsibilities are quite varied. A company is not a machine." What are his takeaways from working on a project? Counting on each finger, he says, "Management is not physics; there are no right answers; really there are different answers; and you have to learn to live with ambiguity." He then adds that IEDC has "stretched my mind" and "shown me how the world really works."

At its best, the case teaching method enables students to develop what Harvard Business School Professor Tom Piper calls "the courage to act under uncertainty." But, in truth, the case method has students *think* about acting under uncertainty. The "action-learning" model embedded in consulting projects forces students to *act* under uncertainty. Interestingly, Harvard is now adopting team- and project-based learning in its pedagogy.

Western support for Management Education in the CEE Region

Even as Danica was reaching out to the West to build her business school from the "bottom up," the West began to reach into the CEE region from the "top down" with funds, technical assistance, and guidance on how to best educate managers. There were, for example, various business school-to-business school partnerships: The State University of New York (SUNY) in Buffalo worked with the Riga Technical Institute to create the Riga Business School in 1992; the University of California, Berkeley helped to launch the Graduate School of Management at St. Petersburg State University in 1993; and countless faculty from schools in the U.S. and Western Europe advised on curriculum, taught courses, and began research projects with CEE schools and faculty.

The U.S. government spent monies on management education through its Support for East European Democracy (SEED) program and USAID (U.S. Agency for International Development) grants to "institutionalize political democracy and economic pluralism" in CEE countries. Nenad, new to IEDC, was one beneficiary. As part of a $50 million USD program that invited 50 business professors from CEE countries to the U.S., he visited at Harvard, Stanford, and the University of Chicago. Though shocked at the costs—averaging $1 million per visiting faculty—he was impressed with the facilities, classrooms, and students at U.S. schools but gave faculty mixed reviews. "It was odd," he recalled, "I asked students who their favorite teachers were and at Stanford and Chicago, they couldn't name anyone. At Harvard, everyone had a favorite, or two and three of them." On this point, it is worth noting that the Harvard Business School puts top priority on good teaching; the business schools at Stanford, Chicago, and elsewhere in the U.S. put far more emphasis on faculty research.

The European Foundation for Management Education (EFMD) also turned its gaze eastward in the 1990s. Started in 1972, the EFMD is a network of business school deans, MBA program directors, executive education administrators, and select companies formed to enhance management education in Europe–meaning Western Europe in its first two decades of operation. By the 1990s, it was sending, from member schools, hundreds of faculty into CEE countries and in 1991 held its annual meeting in Vienna, Austria featuring American management guru Tom Peters.

Institutional Isomorphism?

What was this outreach from the West to the CEE region all about? In a political-economic frame, it was of course about promoting political democracy and capitalism, not to mention hegemony and market expansion, depending on your point of view. Through a more scholarly lens, this institution-to-institution exchange can also be seen as one part of a "Great Transformation," as described by Peter Drucker's friend Karl Polanyi. Free markets, Polanyi points out, are no more "natural" than any other form of an economy. Instead, they are "instituted" or "embedded and enmeshed in institutions, economic and non-economic."

Developing this point, Nina Bandelj, a Slovene sociologist who worked as the first young researcher at IEDC and is now based at the University of California, Irvine contends that CEE business schools became "westernized" through a process known as "institutional isomorphism" whereby organizations become similar to one another. In this case, similarity was primarily achieved via "institutionalization from the outside."

Western donors, for example, funded the launch or makeover of many of the CEE business schools, effecting change by controlling the purse strings (coercive isomorphism). Professional associations like EFMD and its American equivalent exerted influence by either issuing or withholding their "seal of approval," depending on how various CEE schools progressed (normative isomorphism). Finally, she contends, CEE schools themselves also sought endorsement by and affiliation with Western institutions for the sake of legitimacy and esteem; so they imitated them (mimetic isomorphism).

What this analysis leaves out, however, is Danica's selective intent to "take the best from the west, *and leave the rest*." Institutional theory also neglects the power of local culture, pride, and association to resist institutional isomorphism and to enable, in the face of new circumstances, a more culturally-resonant transformation.

They Don't Understand Us!

Tom Peters, son of an evangelist, scholar of corporate cultures, and co-author of the best-selling management book *In Search of Excellence,* traveled from his EFMD meeting speech in Vienna by private jet in 1991. He was met by Danica at the airport, with fresh flowers for his wife, and transported, Danica laughs, by a "big car" because "he's an American, you know." They all toured Ljubljana, sampled sour cabbage at the great vegetable market, and made their way to Brdo where Peters would address an assemblage of Slovene managers, government officials, and dignitaries.

It is ironic, in light of the institutional versus culture theory debate, that Peter's talk was entitled "The American Way of Managing–A Model for the Whole World?" In it, he argued that while accounting was essential to management, Eastern Europeans should not adopt the methods developed in the 1840s that were still in use in the U.S. He also said that finance should be informed by dynamic, not static, models. Peters then made the case that Slovenes could learn a lot about service culture from the U.S., noting that at an American petrol station you could buy fuel, get a car wash, have a cup of coffee, and even purchase groceries or eat lunch. Of course in his analysis of excellent companies, Peters stressed that one comparative advantage is their indigenous or "home grown" culture.

Peter's messages resonated with Danica and he too connected with Slovenia, staying an extra two days to savor the music and mood of Bled and Ljubljana. Nonetheless Danica was still steamed about what was happening in relation to the EFMD. As its first board member from CEE, she tried to convince other board members to "pay bigger attention to CEE, to organize conferences in CEE, to include management students into European competitions, and so on. But none of these suggestions were accepted."

More broadly, she was "frustrated" that the Western European schools were not sending their best faculty to the region. And she was angry about the prevailing attitudes which could be described as condescending. "The EMFD has money to support management development here, but they don't understand the region. We are also European, sophisticated, with an appetite for learning. Many here have a broad education in philosophy, science, and the arts," she went on. "You know, management concepts are not so difficult to learn if you are a well-educated person."

She was not the only one with such complaints. Nancy G. McNulty, of the North American Management Council, in collaboration with Russian professor Alexander Katkov described the "best from the west" situation in 1993 this way: "Too many American consultants and managers are failing in their efforts in Eastern Europe by misjudging Europeans' educational attainments and by ignorance of their life styles, ways of learning, management and teaching methods, and cultural values. Offering 'kindergarten-level' management education, as an outrageous example, leads to resentment that does not lie buried."

Forming CEEMAN

Motivated by all of this, Danica made a decision, "I shall make an association on my own." At the EFMD conference in Vienna, Danica noticed that there were only two other Central Europeans (two Hungarian deans) who participated whereas Central and Eastern Europe together had close to half a billion people. After her several proposals for “Going East” were rebuffed at the EFMD board meeting, she listened to an address by Erhard Busek, then Minister for Science and Vice Chancellor of Austria. As she tells it, “Busek spoke enthusiastically about how important it was for Western Europe to open to the East and to appreciate the quality that CEE has to offer, especially concerning its educated people. He used the same words that I had a half hour before at the Board Meeting!” Afterwards, Danica went to greet Busek and recalls: “This speech helped me make the final decision to create an association that we (in the East) shall be responsible for, that we shall find finances for, and that will help to accelerate management development in CEE.“

In early 1993, after an international conference at Brdo, Danica met with 13 deans from CEE countries and suggested that they establish an association that would cover the region. The idea was met initially with resistance. Some deans, for instance, wanted to affiliate only with the EFMD (including those who envisaged travelling to Brussels and to Paris after their boarders opened--and not to Poland or Slovenia!). Others, recalling years of cross-national conflicts in the Soviet-led Council for Mutual Economic Assistance, wanted no part of any pan-CEE association. At that moment Derek Abell--a “highly credible Western guy” who was by then an advisor on management education to several CEE governments--reminded the deans that the region would “need 2,500 professors in the next decade.” He supported Danica’s arguments for association and convinced the deans to join in.

Later in the year 1993, the CEE deans met in again in Brdo. Andrzej Koźmiński, then head of the International Management Center at the University of Warsaw, Poland spoke out about CEE schools’ “bad habit of mimicking the West.” He argued that without shared learning or a sense of solidarity, individual schools would train technocrats or, worse, turn students into American-style “corpocrats”; whereas the real need for the region was to develop entrepreneurs and leaders. Danica, in turn, stressed the importance of the region having "one voice" on matters of accreditation and quality.

Still there were geopolitical rivalries to contend with: some of the Russians, for instance, wouldn't support locating the association's headquarters in Warsaw or other capitals in the former-Soviet bloc; the Baltic countries and other border states wouldn't countenance an HQ in Moscow or St. Petersburg. The small and "neutral" Slovenia had its advantage in this regard and it was agreed to house the association at IEDC. The name CEEMAN (joining CEE and management) was proposed by an architect, Janez Koželj, who is today vice-mayor of Ljubljana and a professor at the faculty of architecture. Danica invited Koźmiński to become vice-president of CEEMAN to boost its academic credentials and regional identity.

CEEMAN members met the next year in Warsaw for a regional conference on East-West partnerships. At a 1995 gathering in St. Petersburg, to learn from the best-run companies, the CEEMAN brand was formally launched. For Danica, the CEEMAN logo was perfect: Arcing blue lines moving as across water, like ripples from stone, a sign of growing power and influence. "We are stronger and better as partners with other institutions," she remarks.

A conferee at the 1995 conference recalls the Russians laughing with the Poles, even as their politicians were fighting, the Czechs and Hungarians comparing folk songs; and plenty of vodka. When the mayor of St. Petersburg couldn't attend, the deputy mayor, Vladimir Putin, spoke to the delegates instead. Reflecting on these first meetings, Koźmiński marveled at the "synergies between Central and Eastern Europe business schools," and how "CEEMAN created identity and instilled a sense of pride." As Madis Habakuk of Estonia put it, "The major idea is networks. Linking with colleagues from Latvia, Lithuania, and picking up new ideas." Modris Ozolins, from Riga added, "We got confidence. We could do things better than Western consultants."

In the next decade, CEEMAN would launch an academy to develop hundreds of new professors and its ripples would extend well beyond the boundaries of the CEE region. All of this, according to Danica, extended the originating vision. But, who would pay for it?

Enter George Soros

George Tividar was born in 1930 to Jewish parents in Hungary who were deeply concerned with cross-cultural conflict. The family adopted the language of Esperanto—a universal tongue—in hopes of promoting world harmony. At age six, George was given a new last name: Soros, which in Esperanto means to "soar." When the Nazis occupied Budapest in 1944, his father bribed a Hungarian official to claim George as his Christian godson, and the family survived the Holocaust.

In 1947 the Soros family relocated to England, where George attended the London School of Economics. There, he read Karl Popper's 1945 book *The Open Society and Its Enemies* which introduced Soros to the concept and ideal that would shape his thinking and activities for the rest of his life. The term "open society" comes from the French philosopher Henri Louis Bergson who used it to describe societies founded on universal principles deigned to advance the welfare of all mankind, as opposed to a "closed society" that puts self-interest ahead of nation and culture.

Over the next two decades after graduation, Soros moved into international arbitrage—buying securities in one country and selling them in another—in London and later New York City where he befriended Beat poet and new left radical Alan Ginsburg and refined what some characterize as a "radical" perspective on politics and capitalism. By 1990, he had amassed a personal fortune of over $10 billion USD and made $1 billion more during the 1992 Black Wednesday U.K. currency crises. A year later he would create the Open Society Institute which, as part of its philanthropy, spends $500 million annually to, among other things, "encourage transitional and emerging nations to become 'open societies.'" "I realized [as a young man] that it's money that makes the world go round," says Soros, "so I might as well make money.... But having made it, I could then indulge my social concerns."

One of those concerns was to support business and management education in his homeland. In 1988, he helped to found in Budapest the Central and Eastern European business school (then called the International Management Center), in association with Indiana University, where students could receive an American MBA. Shortly thereafter, he offered to financially support CEEMAN's programs to train new CEE faculty and reach out to faculty in developing nations in Asia and Africa.

IEDC Governance and Mission

In its founding, the IEDC was an organizational unit within the Slovenia Chamber of Economy. From 1987 onward, however, it had autonomous governance in the form of a Supervisory Board, composed of influential founding figures and prominent representatives of Slovenian business community. In those days, membership included Dr. Peter Kraljič, Marija Lah, Management Board Director, Petrol Ljubljana, Professor Lojze Sočan, and Horst Weitzmann, a well-known German entrepreneur. The school also had an Academic Advisory Board that included Professors Derek Abell, Hellmut Schütte, Tony Dimnik, Queen's University, Canada, David Kuechle, Harvard University, Pedro Nueno, IESE Barcelona, Spain, Peter Welzel, Augsburg University, Germany, and Peter Rohleder, Managing Partner, St. Gallen Consulting Group, Switzerland.

The main tasks of the Supervisory Body included appointment and review of the director of IEDC, approval of annual reports, budgets, and activities, advisement to management, and oversight of the school's strategic plan. The Academic Board, in turn, counseled the dean, approved the academic program, assisted in faculty recruitment, and advised on academic matters.

What is germane here is their contribution to and oversight of the school's vision and mission. From the start, IEDC was dedicated, first and foremost, to being "an outstanding teaching institution, providing learning with the world's best professors teamed with top regional experts." To affect this, there would be no academic department silos in the school. On the contrary, in-house and visiting faculty would co-operate across disciplinary boundaries and often work together in planning and delivering classes and programs.

Second, the school dedicated itself to developing managers "with the highest of professional and ethical standards." In so doing, IEDC pledged to promote "business as an activity based on a broader humanistic texture, like arts and culture, giving additional meaning to management," and to "respect and incorporate the basic values of our civilization, such as dignity, freedom, participation, solidarity, and subsidiarity."

If all of this sounds a bit legalistic and wordy, it is because it was the byproduct of long dialogue and deliberation between Danica, the Supervisory Body, the Academic Advisors, and the IEDC faculty and staff. There were two other points that Danica insisted be included in the guiding vision. First was that the school position itself as an "agent of change"—for students and managers, for Slovenia, the region, and CEE, and later, for business education and the practice of management. Second was that the school in word and deed embrace her founding maxim: "Only the Best is Good Enough."

"Shock Therapy" for the Yugoslav Economy

In the 1990s, the IMF more or less controlled the Yugoslav central bank. Its tight money policy further crippled the country's ability to finance its economic and social programs. State revenues that should have gone as transfer payments to the republics went instead to service debt. The republics were left on their own to survive. From 1989 through September 1990, more than a thousand companies went into bankruptcy. By 1990, the annual GDP growth rate had collapsed to a negative 7.5 percent. In 1991, GDP declined by a further 15 percent, while industrial output shrank by 21 percent.

The CEE region was undergoing "shock therapy"--the sudden release of price and currency controls, withdrawal of state subsidies, immediate trade liberalization, and privatization of publicly-owned assets. One of its main proponent was Jeffrey Sachs, then a Harvard professor, whose methods had been hailed in the turnaround of Bolivia's economy in 1985. Sachs was an advisor to the Polish government in 1990 which had some eventual successes and later to Russia where shock therapy was also implemented–to dismal results. Russia's economy sank further and Sachs was accused, though never charged, with profiteering through Russian privatization.

Yugoslavia followed this general economic path at the start of the 1990s. Under a new law, for example, if a business were unable to pay its bills for 30 days running, or for 30 days within a 45-day period, the government would launch bankruptcy proceedings within the next 15 days. Nearly 2,500 industrial enterprises were liquidated leaving 1.3 million workers out of jobs. Other socially-owned enterprises survived by not paying their workers. By 1991, real wages were falling dramatically, social programs closed, and unemployment rose.

There was a testy relationship between Sachs and Slovenia during this period. Sachs was abrasive and domineering: He berated the Slovenian parliament for passing a bill without his approval, and dismissed critics as "idiots" and "self-management imbeciles." In turn, World Bank economist David Ellerman, who challenged Sach's prescriptions for Slovenia, remarked, "Only the mixture of American triumphalism and the academic arrogance of neoclassical economics could produce such a lethal dose of gall."

Each of the states of the CEE faced economic hardships in the 1990s and each dealt with its own distinct socio-political and cultural challenges. Yugoslav President Borisav Jović described the mounting tensions in his region this way: "The reforms are having a markedly unfavorable impact on the overall situation in society.... Citizens have lost faith in the state and its institutions.... The further deepening of the economic crisis and the growth of social tensions has had a vital impact on the deterioration of the political-security situation."

Consider, to close this chapter, how a Slovene manager, a graduate of IEDC, coped with the economic collapse in her nation and the lessons she learned about leadership.

Tatjana Fink, Women Leading

"A few months after the end of the course I was promoted to the position of managing director. The MBA program helped facilitate this promotion by giving me a framework to solve problems and for understanding the latest strategies to achieve business goals." This quote, from Tatjana Fink, appears on many IEDC brochures—a promise to prospective students that what they learn at the school can also help them to make it in the business world. How did it work for Tatjana?

First she attended the seven-week General Management Program in 1989 and later the Executive MBA program in 1991. She was enthralled with her experiences with faculties and peers in the program. Consultations with a local business were "just like real life." The class organization also piqued her interest: Seamless movement from a consultation team to cross-team learning forums to the whole class operating as one organism. She applied this "molecular model," as she calls it, to her own company Trimo to connect with business partners and create comprehensive solutions for customers. Today Trimo, where she is the General Manager, sells buildings, facades, roofs, and modular units in more than 50 countries.

Shortly after completing her studies, her firm, like others amidst the financial crisis, was near collapse. Over one half of the metal-processing companies in Slovenia went into bankruptcy during this period. Trimo went into its own version of shock therapy—cutting back sharply but also engaging every employee in proposing ideas and redoubling efforts. A crash program starting with intense customer engagement, then Total Quality Management, and later adoption of the European Model for Business Excellence and moves toward sustainability led to the turnaround of the business.

But there was more to this than performance programs and re-engineering. "We created an innovative atmosphere and encouraged employees to think and act differently." This she credits in part to her experiences at IEDC. At the school, she reflected, we learned about "feeling into the other person." In management parlance, this is referred to as EQ—emotional intelligence—and calls for openness and empathy from an executive.

Leadership Lessons

Tatjana has a tough-minded outlook on leading. "My management style ranges from a completely democratic to completely authoritative style. It depends on the situation," she reports. She also has firm opinions on innovation. Recalling IEDC Accounting Professor Randy Kundar's aphorism, "What doesn't jingle, doesn't count," she has this to say about new ideas: "I have my own definition of innovation in business. It should generate cash. If there is no cash, it is not innovation; it is just an idea or a philosophical thesis. We invest a lot in developing talent but if this does not generate return it is like stashing goods in a warehouse without using them. Therefore, we are doing a lot to motivate people to become real partners."

Trimo's latest innovation is an Urban Crash competition for students of architecture and design. This year's contest was to design a public architectural installation for Nove Fužine, a residential neighborhood in Ljubljana using Trimo materials. Competitors came from all over the globe—reflecting Trimo's newfound worldwide reach. Looking back on her business career, Tatjana remarked to a business publication: "My greatest achievement is definitely the systematic and successful international development of Trimo. This is what I believed in from the beginning, even though at that time the majority was skeptical about it. We succeeded, because we gained a critical mass of the creators of the new story."

Why does she stay so closely connected to IEDC-Bled? "I believe in Danica. She's a born pioneer." The same has been said of Tatjana. Both she and Danica have been rated as the top female executives in Slovenia and role models for younger managers. As women leaders, they have especially made a mark among female students whose various blog entries about the two read: "made me comfortable with myself," "set a strong example," and, simply, "wow." Listen to Yesim Kuscu, an MBA student from Turkey, on what she discovered at IEDC: "Women are strong here. They speak up and speak out." "Maybe," she adds, "even more so than the men."

→ TRAGEDY AND TRANSFORMATION

The smell of freedom had been wafting through the Slovenian air throughout IEDC's early years of operation in Brdo. Students, workers, civil society groups, and free-spirited Slovenes agitated for liberalization and reforms. During the spring of 1986, the 12th Congress of the League of Socialist Youth of Slovenia passed a resolution in support of civil society, referencing environmental, human rights, gay rights, and pacifist grassroots movements in Slovenia. Delegates also demanded freedom of speech, freedom of assembly, and the right to strike.

In 1987, a Slovenian "alternative" journal *Nova Revija* published a collection of 16 articles in favor of an independent and democratic Slovenia. Later that year a strike broke out in Ljubljana with workers demanding political pluralism and the right to establish independent trade unions. In spring, 1988, the Slovenian Peasant Union was formed as the first openly non-Communist political association in Yugoslavia. This was the beginning of the Slovenian Spring—one year before the revolution of 1989 in Eastern Europe and the subsequent collapse of the Soviet Union.

On December 23, 1990, Slovenia held a referendum which passed with 95 percent of the vote in favor of independence. Immediately after these elections, the government in Belgrade invoked the defense doctrine whereby the armies of each of the Republics would come under Yugoslav People's Army (JNA) command. The Slovenian government resisted these moves and secured its military equipment and arms. It also declared that its territorial army would remain under the sole command of the Slovenian government.

10 Day War

Over the next six months, Slovenia set up a secret defense command and mobilized over 20,000 military and police to protect the homeland. Independence was declared June 25, 1991. JNA forces invaded from the east, south, and west and the Yugoslav Air Force dropped leaflets over Slovenia bearing the messages "We invite you to peace and cooperation!" and "All resistance will be crushed."

In the early hours of June 27, the military leadership of Yugoslavia telephoned Slovenian President Milan Kučan to advise him that JNA troops intended only to take over border crossings and the airport. A meeting was hastily convened at which Kučan and the rest of the leaders of the government decided on armed resistance.

Over the course of the 10 Day War, the Slovenian army carried out a guerilla campaign against the larger and more heavily armed JNA. Invading tank columns were trapped when lead and rear vehicles were destroyed as they passed through narrow mountain roads. Lightweight missile systems, purchased secretly from foreign suppliers, repelled airplane attacks and ground troop movements. Two helicopters ferrying JNA soldiers and officers were shot down.

Across Slovenia, skirmishes erupted, some involving heavy fighting, but it was soon apparent that the JNA wasn't fully behind this war and that the Milošević government in Belgrade had far bigger concerns over the declaration of independence by Croatia. A cease fire was declared on July 4, 1990 and a treaty followed two days later whereby Slovenia's independence was agreed and its army and government recognized by Belgrade. Estimates are that the JNA suffered 44 fatalities and 146 wounded, while the Slovenes had 18 killed and 182 wounded.

The IEDC campus at Brdo was not untouched by the 10 Day War. While Danica was out of the country, studying for two months at the International Senior Manager's Program at the Harvard Business School, three Western European professors were teaching for the school as the fighting erupted. Preparing to depart, they learned that the Ljubljana airport was occupied by JNA troops. Fighting was underway on roads throughout Slovenia, too.

René Magdalenić, who was leading a seminar outside of the school in a mountain resort, decided not to leave the country. He spent the entire 10 days walking around the countryside and talking to farmers. He was so touched by the experience that he decided later to study Slovene and today offers courses in the national language when it is so desired.

The other two professors, Hellmut Schütte and Philippe Lasserre from INSEAD, were at the Brdo campus. The radio announced that the last train on which the foreigners could embark was leaving from the border station Jesenice at 2 p.m. Veronika Stabej, a program manager at that time (today Ambassador of Slovenia in France), took the initiative to lead the faculty to the station. They set out by car at 10 a.m., avoiding roadways and following rutted paths through farm fields. At one point, they stopped so that Michele, Philippe's wife, could take a photo of peasants arming themselves for defense. The peasants rushed toward her and Veronika hustled Michele back into the car and raced them away to escape.

As they arrived at the station, the train was pulling away (the normally 30 minute trip taking four hours). Veronika raced to the front of the train and stopped it. The visitors boarded, left the country safely, and afterwards sent a letter about how heartbreaking it was for them to leave Veronika on the platform in Jesenice in such a dire situation. It took Veronika several hours more to return to her home in Ljubljana. She arrived home in tears because she had witnessed a JNA helicopter shot down in front of her.

Danica could not return from the U.S. during the 10 days because the Slovene borders were closed. So she phoned the school regularly, speaking to staff huddled in air raid shelters. She remembers feeling "terribly guilty" about being away from Slovenia in these times and recalls warmly how Milena Fornazarič, a program manager, rallied her peers (and Danica) with reassurance and good cheer. Unable to concentrate on her studies, Danica moved into action by giving an interview to the *Christian Science Monitor* saying that America "didn't do Slovenia a favor" by failing to recognize Slovenia's independence and by calling for Yugoslavia to remain together. This would only encourage more warfare.

Prior to the 10 Day War, there were international concerns about traveling to Slovenia. For example, one professor scheduled to lead a seminar in Brdo called Danica to sheepishly say that the American authorities advised him not to travel to Yugoslavia. Arrangements were made to move the program to a Slovene chapel in Klagenfurt, Austria, and students were transported there. After the 10 Day War, the international airport and railways were opened for travel and campus life settled down a bit. Not so southward in the Balkans.

The Breakup of Yugoslavia

Tito's death, mass movements favoring independence, the collapse of the Soviet Bloc, the economic shocks and their fallout—all of these factors and more contributed to the conflictual breakup of Yugoslavia. Tito had created a structure of weights and balances to maintain a multinational and multiethnic federation of six republics (Slovenia, Croatia, Serbia, Bosnia-and-Herzegovina or BiH, Montenegro, and Macedonia). Yugoslavia also housed two autonomous provinces operating within the political framework of Serbia: Vojvodina, with its sizable Hungarian population, and Kosovo, with a majority Albanian population. After Tito's death in 1980, central power started to devolve, and the communist party became more decentralized.

Marko Bulc had an idea for saving the federation from dissolution. Running for the post of Slovenian representative to the Yugoslav Presidency, he proposed the creation of a kind of "United States of Yugoslavia." Laws were drafted to support Slovenia's move to a market economy. Ten articles were drafted on reconstituting workers' councils, defining the responsibilities of managers, setting up supervisory boards for firms, and so on. But the Slovenian public instead chose Janez Drnovšek, a young economist and a comparatively fresh face, to represent them.

In Belgrade, center of the Yugoslavian government, Drnovšek encountered Serbian communist party head Slobodan Milošević who had gained power inciting Serb nationalism. Drnovšek recalled his meeting: "I once said to Milošević: 'Your policy is like riding a tiger. While you ride it you probably feel very powerful. But sooner or later you'll have to come down and the tiger will eat you.' Alas, I did not succeed in changing his politics or his behavior."

War in the Balkans

Slobodan Milošević became leader of the Serbian communist party in 1987. His rise to power coincided with ethnic tensions in the two autonomous provinces under Serbian control. He accused the leaders of both Kosovo and Vojvodina of alienating Serbs living in their regions. Slogans like "Oh Serbia from three parts, you will be whole again" were popularized through the Serbian media.

On October 5, 1988, some 150,000 people, largely ethnic Serbs, gathered in Novi Sad to protest against the Vojvodina provincial government. The government tried to cut off the power and water supply to the protesters, enraging the assemblage further and swelling the crowd. When the electricity was restored, the provincial government tried to pacify the crowd by distributing bread and yogurt. Soon thousands of yogurt packages were thrown at the Parliament building, an episode described as the "Yogurt revolution" by the media.

In early 1989 Milošević pushed through a new constitution that drastically reduced the autonomy of Kosovo. Hundreds of Kosovo-Albanians were subsequently killed when demonstrations against it were violently suppressed by Serbian security forces.

On June 28, 1989, Milošević delivered a speech at a celebration marking the 600th anniversary of the Battle of Kosovo (between the Christian Serbs and Moslem Turks in the 14th century). He spoke, "Six centuries later, now, we are being again engaged in battles and are facing battles. They are not armed battles, although such things cannot be excluded yet. However, regardless of what kind of battles they are, they cannot be won without resolve, bravery, and sacrifice, without the noble qualities that were present here in the field of Kosovo in the days past...." The speech was warmly received by elements in the ethnically Serbian crowd who were reported to have shouted "Kosovo is Serb" and, more darkly, heralding his hatred of Muslims.

Slovenia's independence in 1991 was tolerated in Belgrade in part because it was mostly Christian and ethnically homogenous. Croatia's declaration of independence that same year was more difficult to accept because a large Serbian minority lived there. And BiH was more complicated still: Serbs, Croats, and Muslims (each a third of the population) were all mixed together. War broke out in Croatia in August, 1991 and in the next year in BiH, spurred by xenophobia and ethnic hatred.

In the Croatian war, Dubrovnik and its surrounds were under siege and bombarded until mid-1992 when that war ended. Roughly one-fourth of the Croatian economy was destroyed. Throughout BiH, Bosnian-Serb nationalists and the JNA began a systematic policy of "ethnic cleansing" to erase all vestiges of the non-Serb populace. Entire villages were destroyed. Thousands were forcibly expelled from their homes, held in detention camps, raped, tortured, deported, or executed. The siege of Sarajevo in Bosnia was the longest in the history of modern warfare, running from April, 1992 to February, 1996.

As a result of the wars in Croatia and BiH, hundreds of thousands were killed. Neither UN resolutions, nor EU-observers, nor a UN "peace-keeping" force could stop the fighting. Only in 1995, when the Americans began to bomb the Serbian positions in Bosnia, did the conflict wind down. Together with increasing Croatian military pressure, this brought an end to the war. The Dayton agreements which followed established a measure of peace and order in BiH. The conflict overall would conclude with NATO bombing and the withdrawal of Serbian forces from Kosovo in 1999.

Milošević resigned the Yugoslav (primarily Serbian) presidency amid demonstrations after a disputed presidential election in 2000. He was arrested by federal authorities on charges of corruption, but the charges faltered and he was sent to stand trial at The Hague for war crimes. Milošević conducted his own defense in the five-year long trial, which ended without a verdict when he died on March 11, 2006 in his prison cell of a heart attack.

On Tragedy and Leadership

Danica recalls flying to Sarajevo on the first plane allowed in from Ljubljana in 1996. "We were all crying as we landed." She was on a mission to design a week long leadership module for senior managers from British Aerospace plc (now BAE Systems) on the theme of organizational transformation. BAE was going through a merger at the time and encountering a corporate "clash of cultures." There was certainly a clash of cultures in Sarajevo so in that sense the setting was well suited to BAE's needs. More than this, going to the war zone would confront the executives with leading under "extraordinary circumstances." Ultimately the seminar would concern the themes of leadership, tragedy, and transformation.

The overall BAE program was the brainchild of Jonathan Gosling, then at Lancaster University in the U.K. and now at the University of Exeter. Jonathan was trained as an anthropologist, worked as a mediator of neighborhood conflicts in London, and later was founding Secretary of the European Conference on Peacemaking and Conflict Resolution. He took a mid-career MBA, entered university teaching, and together with Henry Mintzberg and three other professors created the International Masters in Practicing Management in which BAE executives were early participants.

The program was built around the "five minds of a manager." As Gosling and Mintzberg describe them:

- A *reflective mindset* allows you to be thoughtful, to see familiar experiences in a new light, setting the stage for insights and innovative products and services.
- An *analytical mindset* ensures that you make decisions based on in-depth data––both quantitative and qualitative.
- A *worldly mindset* provides you with cultural and social insights essential to operating in diverse regions, serving varied customer segments.
- A *collaborative mindset* enables you to orchestrate relationships among individuals and teams producing your products and services.

- An *action mindset* energizes you to create and expedite the best plans for achieving your strategic goals. Gosling also refers to this a "catalytic" mindset.

What distinguishes this kind of program from garden-variety management development is not only its roots in the five mindsets but also its experiential components. Participants travel to different lands to encounter local culture; they meet with leaders and managers to hear and share leadership stories; and their learning is based in deep personal and situational reflection.

Amplifying on this pedagogy, Gosling describes three distinct types of management education. The first, *utilitarian*, helps managers run their businesses more effectively. This is the usual stuff in management development programs. The second, *explanatory*, exposes them to the complex systems surrounding their work and has them inquire into what it means to be efficient, effective, and accountable as a leader. This approach, more about raising questions than providing answers, is the exception rather than the rule in management development programs.

A third type is what Gosling terms *cathartic*; he writes, "The process of education (literally 'ideas drawn out from the Soul'--e+ducare) leaves one with a sense of being part of a moral order that is essentially 'just.' Sympathy with the tragic predicaments of those with greatness, yet flawed in very human ways, produces not cynicism or depression, but a sense of value in striving for good."

Gosling, introduced by a colleague, Yves Doz, from INSEAD visited Danica with the idea of designing a cathartic experience for the BAE managers. In her mind, Sarajevo was the obvious locale to have such an experience rooted in local culture. One problem was actually getting the BAE managers to the city. The CIA had issued warnings against travel to the war-ravaged capital. Danica immediately contacted the British ambassador in BiH, who sent a message back to BAE via London that the city was safe and would welcome them. The next challenge was to enlist local leaders who could and would share their leadership stories.

Assembling a Seminar in Sarajevo

The second half of 1992 and first half of 1993 were the height of the siege of Sarajevo, when the city was encircled by a force of 18,000 Serbian troops, stationed in the surrounding hills, from which they assaulted Sarajevo with artillery, mortars, tanks, rocket launchers, aircraft bombs, and sniper rifles. Signs reading Pazite, Snajper! ("Beware, Sniper!") were common and certain dangerous streets were known as "sniper alleys." By the siege's end, it is estimated that nearly 10,000 people were killed or went missing in the city, including over 1,500 children. An additional 56,000 people were wounded, nearly 15,000 of them children.

One of the wounded was Zlatko Lagumdžija who was Prime Minister of BiH when the shelling began. On May 24, 1993, the news from Sarajevo reported, "Bosnian Serbs defied a pledge Saturday and unleashed their most intense attack in weeks. Nine people were killed in Sarajevo and more than 100 wounded, including Bosnia's deputy prime minister." Zlatko would immediately undergo surgery for shrapnel wounds to his thighs, stomach, and legs.

Danica had met Zlatko long before the war when he traveled to Belgrade representing a Bosnian youth organization. Today in his office at Social Democratic Party, he is energized that he has won the recent election for Prime Minister but glum that he cannot occupy the post as yet due to wrangling among Bosnian Croats, Muslims, and Serbs. Why did he agree to join in the BAE seminar? "First I say yes, then I think," he smiles. "Danica says I do too much and then she asks me to do something else."

Then he explains, "Slovenia is not east, and it is not west. IEDC was the first management school in the region. It was worth being there." Theater director and film-maker Haris Pašović, from Sarajevo, also joined the seminar. He gained international acclaim when, in 1993, amidst the bombing, he produced *Waiting for Godot* in Sarajevo with Susan Sontag, the New York based author, political activist, and public intellectual who died in 2004.

Early in that conflict, Sontag referred to the siege as the "Spanish Civil War of our time" and urged U.S. and European military intervention. Her motivations for the production were "not so much because I'd always wanted to direct Beckett's play (although I had), as because it gave me a practical reason to return to Sarajevo....I had spent two weeks there in April, and had come to intensely care about the battered city and what it stands for; some of its citizens had become my friends. But I couldn't again be just a witness: that is, meet and visit, tremble with fear, feel brave, feel depressed, have heartbreaking conversations, grow evermore indignant, lose weight. If I went back, it would be to pitch in and do something."

Haris was out of the country when the Serbian shelling of Sarajevo began. He too wanted to "do something" and traveled back to Sarajevo through an underground tunnel under the airport to work with Sontag. He along with many other directors, artists, and musicians would put on over 400 concerts and performances in underground locales throughout the city during the war.

Haris first met Danica in 1997, in Sarajevo, at the behest of Minister Lagumdžija. His initial reaction to the seminar was "not for me." As he and Danica discussed the power of paradox in leading and in art—whether in the form of freedom versus discipline or in the pairing of hope with fear—he saw the possibilities of others learning about cultural clashes, pluralism, catastrophe, and resilience in his home city. He also, as he described it, fell under her "spell." Haris would join with Zlatko, as well as other artists, political leaders, and business executives to reflect deeply on their own experiences in the war and the broader leadership lessons.

Leadership Lessons under Extraordinary Circumstances

In the Sarajevo program, the BAE managers got the full IEDC "experience." The program commenced with a documentary film on a Sarajevo string quartet that performed more than 100 concerts at different locations, mostly underground, during the war. Then the leader of the quartet entered and played David Wilde's song "Crying for Sarajevo," a melody inspired by one of the most well-known tragedies of the war where people queuing to buy bread in front of a bakery were killed by a Serbian grenade.

Next Haris led everyone in a walk through the city to witness massive rebuilding underway amidst many structures still pockmarked by shelling; they saw single- minaret mosques alongside Christian churches and a synagogue; and they sampled grilled čevapćići (kabobs) and foods prepared according to Muslim halal traditions. They climbed to the top of an overlooking hill, eyeing a beautiful city spread below the mountains known as the "Damascus of the North" in the east and as the "European Jerusalem" in the west. From there they could also see bright white gravestones clustered in neighborhoods, by the thousands, all dated 1992, '93, '94, or '95.

As Danica describes it, Haris filled an explanatory role: showing how people from different ethnic origins who lived together for centuries could be brought into conflict. This surfaced challenging questions for participants about how Milošević– and any other leader for that matter–could generate such hatred and blind obedience among a populace.

Zlatko, in his presentation on "My country, my company, myself--How did we transform?" addressed cathartic themes. He spoke of his wounding and 11 subsequent operations and shared his personal journey to self-awareness. "I believe that the most important thing is to appreciate yourself in the politics. You do not measure success with victory, but with the fight for the things you believe in." Then he pointed to his failings in politics: "For me the knowledge I possess was extremely useful, because I could see a big picture. The problem is that it is very difficult for the public to identify itself with it. The mistake I made was explaining something that the others did not understand. In my communication I lack simplicity."

He talked next about his post-politics careers as a professor of MIS at the University of Sarajevo. "One has to have a vision, even in times when everything around you is falling apart." As he relates it, the war was approaching its end, and he had the idea of founding an Information Technologies Centre at the University. Although the city had no electricity, heat, or water and people were concerned only with basic survival, he started to make plans for a modern IT department with satellite dishes (with support from George Soros).

Just a few weeks after the Dayton agreement was signed, a foreign journalist came to interview him about the situation. She saw students at work on a simulation of the Apollo 13 spacecraft. She told him, "Forget about Dayton, we can make a story about this." She later told him that she had not thought the country had a chance of survival but having seen students engrossed in learning--sitting behind a concrete wall where windows should have been--she realized that BiH might have a chance. What was his lesson from this? He stated that "regardless of how low one is, regardless how bad things look, and if one's quality of life is close to 0 on a scale from 0-100, the only way to claw to 3 or 5 percent is to go for 110 percent. The only way to escape from the pit of misery is to go for 110," he told the BAE execs.

Connecting to the Balkans

Zlatko would reenter politics and retain his appointment at the University–keeping the salary from one job and giving the salary from other to charity. He would also participate in future IEDC programs. "You give something, you get something," was how he described his connection to IEDC. "There are very few places where people from the technical, business, and social worlds interact and learn," he explained, "Leadership is lifelong learning."

At another of the BAE seminars, tensions were running high over the capture and trial of Serbian leaders, and the program was moved to Slovenia. Zlatko's counterpart, Mladen Ivanić, the Prime Minister of Republika Srpska (a part of BiH), was asked by Danica to participate in a panel on transformation. In one electrifying moment he was asked by Danica whether or not Radovan Karadžić, the Bosnian Serb leader, was guilty of war crimes. Ivanić, after some hesitation, said yes, that Karadžić was a war criminal. The audience gasped and many approached him afterwards with tears of gratitude in their eyes. (Karadžić was found hiding in Serbia in 2008, arrested, and put on trial in The Hague for war crimes.)

BAE managers have continued to go to Sarajevo for cathartic reflection in IEDC programs. The experiences surface deep questioning among many–about building weapon systems and about whether or not they are truly "peacekeepers." Managers from a Dutch insurance company also participate in IEDC programs in Sarajevo as did MBA students from IMD for four years in a row.

As part of its own mission to serve the recovering nation, IEDC offers BiH management students admission for one-half of the normal tuition. Adnan Medžedović is a Bosnian who took up IEDC's MBA program. He was in the war, at the front line. He studied mechanical engineering but wanted to also become a manager. He thought of going to the U.S., perhaps to study at Wharton or Chicago, and then maybe on to work for an American multinational. Instead he chose IEDC. His student project at IEDC had been advising a filmmaking couple, Rade Šerbedžija and his wife Lenka Udovički, who live in Los Angeles and run the Ulysses Theatre on Brioni Islands in the Adriatic. This was, he reported, a "complex, challenging, and dynamic project." Today Adnan lives in Sarajevo. He also spends time mentoring and coaching young Bosnians as they enter technical trades. "I've been to war. Your values change in such a situation. Now I want to contribute to Bosnia," he explains.

Developments at Brdo

The wars in the Balkans naturally had spillover effects on IEDC throughout the 1990s. MBA admissions from Croatia, BiH, and Serbia declined significantly as did the number of custom management development programs. Just like in every enterprise in South Eastern Europe, the wars took a toll on IEDC's bottom line.

Professors also recall a certain clannishness among some of the MBAs during this period. While students would intermix ethnically and work collaboratively in their learning groups, at breaks and during meals they would gather with country compatriots to share news of the fighting and talk of family and friends back home. Occasionally distress and anger would be expressed in the classroom—veiled in loud disagreements over a business case or shared openly in personal reflections. Still, as Professor Obłoj recalls it, the school was also a "safe haven" for the students. They could step away from the conflicts and gain some perspective on things. And, even as their countries were at war, students would make "friends with 'supposed' enemies" and could see for themselves a brighter future.

Given declining revenues, economic instability, and geopolitical upset and uncertainty, the standard business catechism advises a manager to hunker down, retrench, cut costs, and reduce risks and exposure. Danica, however, was of a different mind and saw opportunity at hand. Her school's growing notoriety was attracting increasing numbers of students not only from all of the CEE countries, but also from Western Europe and even Japan and China. During the conflict years in the Balkans, IEDC received from the Dutch government a major grant to educate human resource managers and had delivered nine programs for more than 200 of them. It led three-week seminars on "How to Do Business with Germany" in cooperation with the Chamber of Munich, Germany. It also organized an international conference on "How to Do Business with Slovenia" in Trieste, Italy, in cooperation with *The Economist*, and held a seminar on strategic alliances for Electrolux-Zanussi, Italy.

In 1996-97, IEDC expanded its roster of customized company programs. It organized a European-wide seminar for personnel managers of Hewlett Packard, two seminars for top management of Pliva, the leading pharmaceutical company in Croatia, a seminar for top management of Agrokor, Croatia, and seminars for the top management of Gorenje of Slovenia and Krka Pharmaceuticals.

All of this indicated IEDC's potential to grow in its reach and its impact. The problem was that the school had outgrown its facilities in Brdo.

Scouting a New School Locale

The facilities at Brdo were not designed for management education. As Professor Ellert described, the classrooms were long and narrow, rather than wide and deep, the preferred configuration for case teaching. There were only a few break-out rooms for small group meeting. And, in any case, the campus was too small to handle an increasing numbers of students and executive programs.

Danica had made wholesale changes in staffing and operations at Brdo in her first 10 years. Besides bringing in new faculty, she had also brought in new administrative staff--speaking multiple languages and being ready to work hard. In its prior operations, works hours at the school started at 7 a.m. and ended at 3 p.m. in keeping with local factory schedules. Danica insisted that school instead operate on 8-to-5 European time–as a signal of its international reach and professionalism to the business community and to the general public. This shift caused some grousing and earned her a few "cold shoulders."

That said, certainly some of the Brdo staff were up to new challenges. Take the resourceful Margita Hafner, member of administrative staff. As Danica tells it, "When a professor asked us if we had a pointer, and I replied (not really knowing), 'Of course we have one,' Margita stood up, went outside and took the antenna off her car and brought it in, saying: "Here is the pointer!" Margita's daughter Uršula works today at the school as a marketing manager.

Another problem at Brdo was that neither catering nor amenities were up to international standards at the start. Before one banquet, for instance, Danica noticed that some of the glasses, plates, and flatware were still soiled or spotted. Calling this to the attention of the catering manager, she received a shrug of the shoulders. That evening, at each place setting, linen napkins were folded beautifully in the shape of a swan, but there were no glasses, plates, or utensils. While services improved over the years at Brdo, IEDC did not run the facility's food-and-lodging operation and could not, as one insider put it, count on its "efficiency" or "effectiveness."

Starting in 1996, Danica began scouting for a new home for her school. She looked first at the possibilities of building on the Brdo grounds. Then she and the architect toured 10 or 15 other locales near or around Ljubljana, including castles, manor houses, and grand hotels, not finding any of them wholly suitable. Finally, she received an invitation from the Mayor of Bled, a beautiful place in the Julian Alps, some 55 km northeast of the capital of Slovenia and 38 km from the international airport, to move the school to the shores of the Lake Bled. Bled offered many attractive features, including plenty of lodging and restaurants, access to alpine skiing, woodland hiking, boating and a world-class rowing center, a luxury hotel (another former residence of Tito) plus a restored medieval castle overlooking the lake. But the facilities that the mayor proposed to Danica were not sufficient for the school's needs (today they house the library, two guest apartments, and student work rooms).

A Modern Monastery

Then Vojteh Ravnikar, a prize winning Slovene architect who was later commissioned to design the new school, discovered that another manor house, Villa Mežakla, right next to one that the mayor proposed, was going on sale. "We acted quickly and we bought it," Danica reports. "As it was a cultural monument we had to take care that the new building, erected on the same place, kept the main features of the old one. Vojteh was leading the process, and he designed together with architect Robert Potokar our first two houses."

On January 7, 2000, the new facilities were opened for students. Two buildings featured modern amphitheatres for case teaching, seminar rooms for large- and small-group activities, a great gathering space opening on to a large terrace, a library and the latest in IT equipment and services. At the opening, and many times thereafter, Vojteh came to lecture about "architecture as an expression of identity" and explained that the inspiration for the design of the newly named IEDC-Bled facility came from Mondrian paintings.

An article in the *Financial Times* compared IEDC with two other beautiful schools, Chicago Graduate School of Business and Imperial College Business School in London, and gave the Bled campus an apt description by calling it "a modern monastery."

Transforming IEDC

Moving to Bled was the capstone of a decade of progress for IEDC. From 1990 to 2000, the number of full-time employees doubled, international faculty partners increased to 70, and the cumulative number of students and corporate participants in IEDC programs rose to 21,000. The number of international (non-Slovene) students and participants in programs increased from 14 percent to 60 percent over the 10 years. As an initial step toward international credentialing, IEDC was one of the two first schools in the region to receive International Quality Accreditation (IQA) from CEEMAN (and later accreditation from the Association of MBAs).

In 1997, the IEDC Supervisory Board was reconstituted in anticipation of a move to Bled. Several more corporate members were added to the Board as "shareholders" in recognition of their financial contribution to the purchase of the campus and outfitting of the new buildings. A new legal entity was created to ensure transparency over the handling of their contributions and IEDC-Bled School of Management was legally reborn as a limited liability company.

Additions to the Supervisory Board were Metod Dragonja, the then General Manager of Lek Pharmaceuticals, Mirko Kaluža, Director, Slovenian Insurance Association, Bruno Korelič, the then Chief Executive, Luka Koper, Anton Majzelj, the then Managing Director, Mobitel, Tatjana Fink, General Manager, Trimo, and Franjo Bobinac, President of the Board, Gorenje. Dragonja was the president of the Supervisory Board and Derek Abell, the vice-president. Peter Kraljič continued to have an important role in the board. Professors John Stopford, London Business School and Rasto Ovin, Faculty of Economics, University of Maribor, were added to the Academic advisory.

Meanwhile, the Slovenian economy gathered steam from 1995 to 2000, trade and tourism increased, and the nation's GDP climbed to and then well above pre-war levels. The annual President's Forum speeches, in turn, addressed forward looking themes. Pedro Nueno, building on Peter Drucker's 10th anniversary message, spoke to managers on self-development and "maintaining your personal value." John Stopford, harkening back to Derek Abell's message that the country would succeed based on brains, rather than brawn, spoke of the challenges of a knowledge economy. The key to success was for a firm to translate organizational knowledge into strategic innovation.

Opening the new campus at Bled, IEDC introduced a revised mission statement. It read:

> The mission of the IEDC, as an agent of change and a learning partner, is to attract the most promising executive and top managers, provide them with world-class management education and other relevant services in a truly international context, inspire them for life-long-learning and prepassre them to act and add value as competent and responsible transformational leaders in their organizations and society at large.

Proudly present was Franjo Bobinac, new Supervisory Board member, enacting that mission at Slovenia's Gorenje Group.

Franjo Bobinac, Innovation and Design

Franjo Bobinac, born 1958, moved into the Management Board in 1998 and was named second in command to the much loved President Jože Stanič of the Gorenje Group, a manufacturer and retailer of home appliances—refrigerators, cookers, microwaves, televisions, and such--based in Slovenia. The strategic aspects of his job were daunting. Wars throughout the region had closed off segments of its traditional markets. Competitors from Turkey were entering the region and offering kitchen appliances for lower prices. And top quality European brands like Merloni, Electrolux, and Bosch and Siemens Hausgeräte (BSH) were on offer for higher-end consumers.

Reflecting on the series of challenges, Franjo remarked, "First we had to survive. Then we had to consolidate our production. Next we had to work on our brand since you cannot build a name if you have problems in your production." A graduate of the Faculty of Economics in Ljubljana in international economic relations, with an MBA from École Supérieure de Commerce in Paris, and having been a general manager in Gorenje's French operations, Bobinac also knew that the company faced a fundamental strategic choice: merge with one of Europe's bigger players or try to go it alone.

Three factors shaped his strategic decision. A first consideration was the impact of being acquired on employees: "There are some values that are appreciated here, and the challenge is to hold on to these values. That is what makes us a family. Remember that Gorenje has been here since 1950 and the history of the company is alive in its employees. Many parts of the company are the lifetime work of some of the workers and managers still in leading positions. We have made a lot of personal sacrifices and do not want that taken by someone else."

A second question had to do with keeping up to date with technology: "Development of household appliances is a never-ending story due to continuous improvements in the field of technology and the changing needs and expectations of home appliance users. Immediately after a generation of appliances has been developed and launched on markets, development of the next generation starts."

And a third question had to do with brand awareness and differentiation. Could Gorenje compete on design with the "big guys?"

Over the next five years, these questions were answered. The company retained its independence, though co-manufactured with its competitors, set up an in-house research-and-development function, and partnered with the Italian designer Pininfarina to enhance its products' functionality, look, and feel. Bobinac became CEO in

2003 and made key acquisitions in Holland and Sweden to expand its reach. Today, 95 percent of its products go to export throughout Europe and abroad.

Leadership Lessons

Bobinac took a seven-week course in IEDC Bled to hone his strategic outlook and, as one of his employees put it, to enhance his "human skills." It was his "first time with this kind of education." He relished learning from the international faculty and interacting with fellow students from different lands and cultures. He also got a keener sense of the importance of ethics, vision, and values in running an enterprise.

The firm has adopted a new set of values as it has grown to over 10,000 employees that exports to 70 countries worldwide. They form the acronym POLCA: probity, openness, loyalty, creativity, ambition. On this latter ambition—"To become the most original, design-minded creator of home appliances devoted to sustainable development and able to flexibly adapt to customers' needs"--the company is today working with the French designer Ora-Ito, the "enfant terrible of industrial design," to introduce "simplexity" in its products. Commenting on their launch, the designer stated, "Personally I like the material treatment and the quality of the finishes. I think that consumers will fall for their intriguing beauty and will enjoy their functionalities. Complex technologies are hidden behind a minimalist façade and that is exactly what makes the product look elegant. People will also like the fact that each product is easy to understand and to live with. They are not complicated to use and for me that is very important. Not only because I am a poor cook, but because I love simplicity." As for sustainability, many of Gorenje's newer appliances feature green "eco-friendly" certifications for energy efficiency and, in the case of washing machines, for lower water consumption.

Bobinac has kept a strong connection to IEDC, staying an active member of its Supervisory Board, and regularly meets with students and fellow executives in classes and special events. He sees the networks created by the school as an invaluable resource. Proudly leading a tour through his firm's showroom, he points out design innovations and then remarks how pleased he was that IEDC moved into its new headquarters in Bled: “the building is a benchmark for Slovenia.”

→ THE ART OF MANAGEMENT DEVELOPMENT

What is it like being an MBA student at IEDC in Bled? Listen to one student describe her experience: "The MBA jungle was really hard... day after day new tasks were given, demanding quests had to be accomplished, blood spilling conflicts to be solved. But my classmates--the 'marvelous 36'--never surrendered! They never surrendered in front of the accounting shaman Randy Kudar or the marketing matador Joe Pons or the strategy terminator Nenad Filipović ...."

There is some poetic license in this description, to be sure, but in key respects education is akin to theater. It features a stage, the classroom and school environs; a script, the way a program and its lessons unfold; scenes involving the dramatization of managerial challenges and dilemmas; and of course performers, including faculty and students.

Now in the traditional classroom, students are often treated like an audience, that is passive watchers or, in the academic sense, vessels to be filled with the professor's wisdom. In management education, however, students are instead part of the cast: co-creators of knowledge and important actors in the educational experience.
Finally, there is a backstage–marketers, accountants, administrators, and such, plus the all-important stage hands and production crew without whom there can be no stagecraft or stimulating learning "performance."

The Performing Stage: IEDC-Bled

When IEDC moved to the new premises at Bled, Danica and her Boards added a new tenet to the school's mission: "A creative environment for creative leadership." The new school was designed as an art gallery where managers and leaders could find inspiration among the works of art of well-known Slovenian and international artists.

Enter the side of the main building, from the parking lot, and you confront a "Golden Era," a set of floor-to-ceiling doors surrounded by red-and-black panels filled with a pastiche of images of politicians, a bear, mystical symbols, and various recycled ready-mades. The artists, five of them known altogether as Irwin (a term connected to Marcel Duchamp) rose from the punk and graffiti fringe in Ljubljana to form the New Slovenian Arts collective together with musicians and a theatrical group. This is to emphasize their collective creativity and shift the emphasis away from any individual artist. Their motif is called "retroavantgardism"–because it looks both backward ("retro") and forward ("avant-garde").

Continue to the main lobby, look left, and you see two sights. In the distance is the beautiful Lake Bled, giving the school one of its taglines, "The School with a View." Closer in are large, grayish paintings of windows from old homes and barns by the Bosnian artist Safet Zec. A leading figure in the "poetic realism" tradition in his country, Safet's home village was destroyed in the Balkan wars in the 1990s and his studio, filled with engravings and copper plates, was burned down. Today his work is found in galleries and museums all over the world. And the works of some well-known contemporary painters Andrej Jemec, Janez Bernik, Jože Ciuha, Vladimir Makuc, Metka Krašovec and others make the main salon a beautiful place.

Climb up the stairs to offices and you find a free gestural landscape painting by Croatian Edo Murtić and a homey country scene of a father showing mushrooms to his son by Slovenian naive artist Konrad Peternelj. If abstraction is more to your taste, look on a table and there's a polished bronze sculpture knifing upward, by Negovan Nemec. In Danica's office is an oil painting of Lake Bled, by Tone Kralj (1929), whose highlight is the small island in the middle of the lake that is home to a church where visitors ring its bell for good luck. Before the church was built, there was a temple here consecrated to Živa, the Slavic goddess of love and fertility.

There are also paintings by faculty and friends of faculty at IEDC. Two oils by Nancy Adler, a leader in the arts and leadership program at IEDC and throughout academe, are found in one office. In another, there is a work by Mrs. Veronica Gosling (the mother of Jonathan Gosling) that Danica favored on one of her trips to the U.K.

Outside of Danica's office is Barbara Vilfan, her "right arm" who serves a Head of the Dean's Office and Operations, and Tanja Grilc, Office Manager. Head back down to the lobby and you find Matjaž Oberstar, a jack-of-all-trades who runs the school's reception desk and ensures that the Illy espresso maker keeps up with student demand. This day, students from throughout Europe are attending their first MBA classes. In the evening, they will put on a performance. The Croats, several in traditional dress, offer Croatian goodies to fellow students and demonstrate typical country dances. The Slovenes, dressed in their traditional attire, also offer local wine and show a YouTube film about "what to do" in their home country. There is considerable debate, as the evening wears on, about which of the two countries' wines are superior. The French, Spanish, Italian, and Greek students, in good humor, claim that wines from their nations are far better.

Front-Stage: Marketing Matador

"Good teachers," intones Joe Pons, "have to be in love with education. You are either passionate about it, or you are mediocre." Putting it into perspective he adds, "It is difficult to find such teachers in the modern business school."

José Pons, his given name, was for 14 years a Marketing Professor at IESE International Graduate School of Management in Barcelona. He is currently head of AXIOMA Marketing Consultants, a firm specializing in strategic marketing projects and in executive development programs concerned with improving a company's customer orientation. He has been a visiting faculty at IEDC since 1997.

Joe learned the craft of case teaching decades ago from Harry Hansen, of the Harvard Business School's International Teacher's Program. As Joe was teaching a case in a "practice" class, Harry prepared a "64 point critique of my presentation. What are you trying to do? Where are you leading the students?" Joe explains that a business case "tells a story. The blackboard provides a structure to organize ideas." His preference is to "start from the end of the case. That creates excitement."

Why is Joe called the matador? The Spaniard first leads the class in one direction and then takes them in another. In an IEDC master class in Sarajevo, some 150 Bosnians, Croats, and Serbs await his red cape. The men, most aged 30 to 45, are in suits. The women are well dressed and slightly younger. It is standing room only. Joe explains that the class will be conducted in English: "Latin is language of medicine. Greek is language of mathematics. English is language of management."

"What makes a manager different?" Joe starts out, "Is it a secretary, the size of the office, or the salary? No, what makes managers different is that they make decisions about allocating resources to activities with goals." He then works them through a marketing case. The presenting problem is that a previously successful sales manager is failing under a new boss. The sales manager believes in staying "close to the customer"–doctors, nurses, hospital staff–and has succeeded by satisfying them irrespective of company product marketing priorities. The new boss wants him to hew closer to the firm's strategic aims. The Sarajevo class at first favors the sales manager and then his boss. Joe keeps probing them, "Should the company want its salesforce to be more like freestyle 'artists' or follow-the-rules 'robots'?"

Afterward, Nermin Kadrić, an IEDC graduate and sales manager for a generic drug maker in Bosnia, shakes his head. "It is very tough competing against European drug companies; like Joe asked, are we competing by imitation or differentiation?"

Orchestration: The Henkel Program

Henkel, headquartered in Dusseldorf, Germany, markets leading brands in home-and-personal care such as Persil laundry detergent, Pril washing liquid, Dial shower and hand soap, Schwarzkopf & Henkel cosmetics and salon products, plus caulks, adhesives, and sealants. The company's HR director in CEE, Zuzana Halkova (at that time management development director), was concerned that the company was not paying enough attention to management development needs in her region. The CEO of the company in Slovenia that Henkel had acquired a few years before recommended that she consider IEDC in Bled as a development platform.

"Tailor-made" management development programs were a growth area for IEDC from 1991 to 2000. Now, with world-class facilities, it could further its engagement with companies and compete with Europe's top business schools in the corporate executive education market. This competitive context was different. As Nenad tells it, the "sale" is not so much about the financial outlay, but rather has to do with the costs in company managers' time versus their attitudes about the experience.

He enumerates the customization components at Henkel: 1) Relevant, appealing content; 2) Tailored to the client's context; 3) Different models and approaches to learning; 4) HR present at every meeting; and 5) Company senior management participates. Prior to the launch of the first program, Zuzana insisted on meeting and seeing each of the program faculty in action.

Nenad's work in this arena is to design and orchestrate appealing management development programs for executives. His goal: that participants don't feel that they "have to come" to a program, but rather that they "want to come." In assembling the performers for Henkel, he cast Joe Pons in a lead role. When working executives in the classroom, Joe has a firm motto, "I respect you, but I don't necessarily respect your ideas." Henkel's marketing department positions its brands as a "friend" to the consumer. Joe challenges the Henkel managers about what "friendly" means in terms of price points and a brand's functional and social benefits; and also asks: "for which consumer niches exactly?"

Playing off Joe is Juan Serrano, a colleague from Barcelona. He plays the "good cop" for executives, at least compared to Joe's "bad cop" in the classroom drama. Rather than analyze a case with the Henkel managers, Juan has them "think from the stomach." He uses films to create "teachable moments." From *Titanic*, Juan notes how the director draws your eyes to lovers in the foreground while an iceberg looms in the background. "What are you watching?" he asks the managers. He uses the Canadian film *Seducing Dr. Lewis* to show how a remote village attracts a medical doctor to its locale. This opens up discussion of customer-centricity at Henkel.

The rest of the cast includes a Croat on finance, a Pole on strategy, and Nenad using "juicy cases" to tee up presentations from the managers on change projects they want to lead at Henkel. An open discussion with Henkel's regional general manager on beating Procter & Gamble rounds out the week-long program.

Does it work? After the initial success, Henkel now comes two-to-three times a year to IEDC in Bled and has a one-year waiting list of applicants. Dining with its managers at Castle Bled, one finds folks of 15 different nationalities who start to share the same language about marketing, strategy, and leadership and who are networked closer to peers and senior managers in the region.

Backstage: The Dream Team

There is some disagreement among the three MBA Coordinators, Iva Eibel, Barbara Ferjan, and Maja Medja Vidic, as to whether they are best called the "Dream Team," in honor of the Olympic basketballers, or Trio Casio, the U.K. street performers of YouTube fame. It seems to depend on their generational differences. Iva came to IEDC from IBM in 2003. She remembers her job description as "First to arrive, last to leave." She was attracted by the international environment and opportunity to work with school alumni. Barbara and Maja are more recent hires.

What do they do backstage? "Everything!" For students that means help with visas, course materials, assignments, and such and for professors, with their syllabi, accommodations, power point presentations, sound system, and so on. In other words, "You are in our hands." "Sitting in the classroom," Maja says, "you look around. You have a mental checklist: is it too hot, too cold, is the sun shining on the projector screen, is the computer working ok?" Iva adds, "We're a walking data base–of people, professors, needs, interests, wives, husbands, and the like."

The trio plays a very important and personal role with students: "Many students have been working in business for some years. Being here is not the same as being home. They discover things about themselves and sometimes they confide in us." "At the same time, you have to be firm–about exams, assignments, and showing up on time—otherwise they don't take us seriously." "We're like their big sisters," says Iva, adding, "but we sometimes have to remind them that we're not their secretaries."

The job also entails trouble-shooting and crisis management. On Barbara's first day of work, for example, a student died of illness overnight, and she moved into action. Fortunately, Faris Gavrankapetanović, an MD and Professor of Medicine, was on the Bled campus, sharing with a group of executives his reflections on treating the wounded during the siege of Sarajevo. Faris was rushed to the MBA classroom where he facilitated a reflection session among the students, an outpouring of grief.

A student gets in a fight in town; two students get divorced and marry one another: "there is always some drama in the MBA class." "You have to be a 'Jane of all trades,'" says Iva, and the team chimes in "electrician, mechanic, IT specialist, hotelier." "If the internet goes down, you're the one who shows her face to the students." The trio has a rule that when their office door is closed, it means one or another in inside hollering or crying. "But, if you are unhappy, you never show it to the students or professors."

Their high point? Graduation. "For two weeks, it's 6 a.m. to 2 a.m. The whole school pitches in. You feel proud. And then we all go drinking in an Irish pub."

"Walking the Grass"

Tadeja Omovšek, Tina Prevodnik, Tina Oblak, Sandra Lisietzky, and Manca Debeljak are backstage for executive education programs. Tadeja came to IEDC 14 years ago, when it was still located at Brdo. Her first workshop was a "hard landing." At that time, she recalls, "there were no cell phones and email on the campus." Joe Pons arrives at the airport very late at night. His luggage has been misplaced including the teaching materials for his program. Tadeja spends the night typing up a short summary of the cases that Joe will teach while he fills flip charts with key points and questions. The next morning it is all improvisation, she says, and it works beautifully.

How does their work differ from that of the MBA coordinators? There are many similarities, but executive participants have "extremely high expectations." Many of them have been to programs at IMD, INSEAD, and other top schools. So at IEDC, "they expect more" and "they get more." It is all about "personal service."

Manca joined the executive program team three years ago to coordinate the General Manager's Program. "Danica told me," she recounts, "be kind and at the same time stay formal. You are the boss. But you have to earn the participant's trust." Manca says that she does her work "not just for the school, but for personal satisfaction. I want our participants to leave here happy."

Gazing out the balcony over Lake Bled, one of the coordinators spots a mute swan moving swiftly across the water. She says, "You know, we're like the swans on the lake. On the surface, we seem to be moving smoothly, but underneath, we're padding our feet like mad."

The two teams take collective responsibilities for an important school ritual. They "walk the grass" into every class session and program. Looking around the school, you see several white planters with lawn grass growing from them, tall and evenly trimmed. "We clip it every day." It was originally thought that every IEDC student would maintain an individual planter--as a sign of their growth and development. "Hah!" say the coordinators, "that didn't work out." But they have kept the tradition alive and walk grass planters to-and-from classrooms at day's start and end. The grass, they say, "symbolizes the growth of managers."

Program Innovations

News note: CNN ranks Lake Bled among the top 12 most beautiful lakes in the world. In the summer, the village is crowded with tourists who come to hike, swim, fish, and boat. They are apt to see 80 plus aspiring and current young managers, from more than 20 countries, sculling across the lake in a team building exercise in IEDC's Young Manager's Program. The two week program features a mix of introductory modules on general management and skill-building sessions on communication, presentations, and leading teams. Says participant Marco Sedia, from Italy, "In certain moments of life it is important to stop and reflect. It happened to me at Bled and the result is that I found out how to build my future. Just like a sudden inspiration, all the activities opened my mind and heart."

In 2002, the school dove deeper into the student market by launching a nine-day Discover Management Program for university students. The program's promotional material reads: "Are you: curious to learn new things and have fun? Interested in management and developing your business skills? Eager to establish networks with colleagues from all over the world? Ready to spend part of your summer at a beautiful Bled?" The key word in this program is discover: the students form and run a business in a week-long simulation. In so doing, the fifty-plus participants learn business basics plus how to work with peers from different nationalities and cultures and a good deal about themselves.

As J.B. Kassarjian, Professor of Management at Babson, describes its development, "Danica gave me a clean slate and I went crazy for a week designing this program which is based on case studies and interactive teaching." The program attracts "all sort of people but they have one thing in common: they are young, smart, ambitious, and want to do something in the world." As graduate Simona Marcu of Romania describes it, "An exciting number of nationalities putting their minds together." Another reports, "I learned how to work and behave as a member of a group, to sacrifice personal interests and to combine knowledge and skills to reach a common goal."

Meanwhile, IEDC worked with CEEMAN to introduce several new programs to develop faculty in CEE countries and beyond. As she assumed leadership, Danica spelled out her vision of CEEMAN "as a global association with its focus on management schools in economies in transition, helping them become high-quality institutions...with each of them having a profile that responds to the specific needs of the environment where the school operates. With its emphasis on innovation I also see CEEMAN as a real contributor to the world treasury of management education."

From 2000 onward CEEMAN grew to 192 members from 48 countries by expanding its reach throughout Asia and the southern hemisphere. "Many schools in developing economies face challenges similar to those we face, and they appreciate CEEMAN's efforts to find solutions," reports Milenko Gudić, the managing director of IMTA, the CEEMAN Teacher's Academy based in IEDC. "We are moving away from being a regional-based to an issue-based association," he reports. That means new programs to "educate educators, promote international research and case writing, and strengthen managerial and leadership capabilities in business schools."

IMTA-International Management Teachers Academy

"Those who can - do. Those who can't - teach. Those who can't teach - teach teachers." This witticism is from Professor Randy Kudar, Emeritus of the Ivey School of Business, University of Western Ontario, Canada, and faculty at IEDC where he is known as the accounting shaman. He also develops teachers with Professors Ellert, Pons, Obłoj, and Kassarjian, already introduced, and Arshad Ahmad, of Concordia University, Montreal, Canada, in a signature program launched by CEEMAN in 2000: the International Management Teachers Academy (IMTA).

IMTA, co-sponsored by the Open Society Institute (Soros supported) and IEDC, runs a two week program in the summer in Bled to prepare junior faculty, initially from CEE countries, to teach in the field of management. Week 1 focuses on general aspects of management education, with special emphasis on teaching methodology--the case method and how to support students' project work. Week 2 divides the young faculty into one of four teaching tracks: Strategic Management, Marketing, Finance, or Leadership and Change Management. As of today, 400 participants from 120 institutions in 33 countries have attended this program.

"I don't know of another course like this. It's a gem," reports Jason Cope, a 2003 IMTA alumnus, "To have so many distinguished professors to ourselves for two weeks--it's unheard of in academia." Adds Ekaterina Sumarokova of the State University of Management, Russia, about what she gained: "New wings for flying!"

Gudić traces the program's roots to the gap throughout CEE and other developing economies between growing market demand for MBAs and management development and a shortage of faculty who could teach in a "modern way." Amidst today's turbulent global change, he sees a need for a "new managerial and leadership paradigm." On the content side, young faculty are exposed to not only management theory, but also the arts and sciences. On the instructional side, they are encouraged to "experiment" with new teaching styles and approaches. What does the faculty educate educators about?

Kudar stresses that teaching is not an "ivory tower" occupation, but rather a central part of a management's school's value proposition for MBAs and executives alike. Among the lessons he imparts to his charges:

- Teaching is a critical element of our value proposition to candidates for our programs. They have come to learn, to develop new capabilities, to become better managers, and to grow as individuals. We talk about training leaders for the future, about making an impact globally, about improving organizations--all of this can be facilitated through outstanding teaching.
- It is impossible to teach what you do not know. Clearly one has to have a mastery of the subject or topic in order to teach it. But mastery implies more than that. Outstanding teachers know how to organize and present their material such that it flows logically and has...validity to the student. The classic saying in this area is that the outstanding teacher makes the complex simple rather than making the simple complex.
- Outstanding teachers also emphasize learning as a process, they work to make learning a pleasurable experience, and they provide clear and quick feedback to facilitate improvement and development by students.... In the case of teaching managers and executives, they are aware that executives do not sit, listen, and read all day long. Thus the

> outstanding teacher knows that it will be necessary to engage the managers in dialogue as an integral part of the learning process

He leaves the young faculty with this vocational message: "The students don't care how much you know until they know how much you care."

Research: Rigor or Relevance?

There is today considerable questioning and controversy over the "modern" model of research that is promulgated in business schools today. Randy Kudar expresses the historic perspective this way, "Business education is a professional and applied discipline similar to engineering, law, and medicine. Academics are well trained to look at conceptual issues and to utilize rigorous methodologies, but the business market is interested in practical solutions to real problems. This implies that research has a different role in business education than in the arts and sciences." By comparison, the competing view is that the management scholar's primary job is to contribute to a body of theory and knowledge irrespective of its relevance to the practice of management.

What is indisputable is that the modern business school has been transformed from a kind of guild hall where practical professors passed on their knowledge to students into a highly competitive, research-driven enterprise. How did this come about? Briefly, starting with the Ford Foundation's influential report in the late 1950s, which chided business educators for being too vocational and lacking a sound scientific basis, business schools have put enormous amounts of time and money into becoming theory- and research-based institutions. They have hired and promoted scholars who draw on the literature and research methods of established academic disciplines (e.g., economics, sociology, psychology); and faculty publications in top- tier, theory-oriented, peer refereed journals have become, as former president of the Academy of Management Tom Cummings puts it, the "gold standard and primary determinant of a business school's prestige." While this model started in the

U.S., it has since become the template for schools in the U.K., South Africa, Canada, and Australia, and increasingly in Europe, Latin America, and Asia.

As a consequence, academic theorizing about business and its leadership has become more distant from practice, research rigor has been emphasized over relevance, and university-based academics themselves spend little time interacting with and learning from practitioners and companies. It has reached the point where many business schools have to employ non-tenured clinical faculty or tap business people as adjuncts to teach students who expect their professors to at least know something about business and its operations. And when it comes to executive education, Professor Obłoj points out, schools typically hire in management consultants.

Is there a right approach to management research in CEE countries? Obłoj observes that while "nobody cares about how and what you teach" in the U.S., so long as you do research, "here in CEE and Russia we have been at the other end of the spectrum. We were doing consulting, improving our teaching skills, and did not pay enough attention to research." As for Western Europe, he goes on tongue-in-cheek, faculty "are neither very good researchers nor very good teachers but they strive to achieve both."

This is not simply a philosophical question for a management school—it also has to do with a school's ranking and reputation, with student and faculty recruiting (and retention), and with accreditation. Both the EFMD and to an even greater extent the AACSB (the American-based Association to Advance Collegiate Schools of Business whose reach is extending globally) put a premium on discipline-based research as opposed to scholarship aimed at practice or management education.

What are the implications for faculty hiring, development, and promotion, and for the faculty culture at management schools in CEE countries? In a round table discussion, the IMTA faculty acknowledge that research and scholarship is an individual decision—for faculty and for schools. But each has a point of view on the ideal professor.

Kassarjian contends that the ideal professor is like a "cocktail with a number of different ingredients—tasting a little sweeter or bitter depending on who does the tasting." But, in his mind, the core ingredient is "first-hand business experience," earned either as a practitioner or a consultant. Obłoj contends that a professor should be a good researcher—"you have to train your brain and keep close to new concepts"—but adds, "at the same time you have to be close enough to business practice to understand how to move these concepts into the classroom." Ellert, in his turn, stresses relevance—in what professors choose to study and how they ultimately communicate their findings. "Participants who enroll in a management degree or continuing education program expect rigorous but practical and relevant content that addresses local and regional concerns, challenges, and business opportunities."

IMTA incorporates these diverse views into a Research and Publishing program for young faculty held at IEDC. It consists of a three-day preparatory seminar that features guidance on defining a relevant research issue, research design and methodology, and research execution and field work. Participants critique each other's research proposals in small groups and get individual mentoring from faculty advisors. They then undertake five months of field research, submit draft research papers, and propose how to integrate their findings into educational material. Afterwards, they return for a two-day workshop where they present their papers, get advice on content and publication potential, and try a hand at teaching what they have found.

In this same spirit, IMTA launched a Case Writing Module through IMTA and annually hosts a Case Writing Competition with Emerald Publishers. One of the role models for budding case writers is Professor Lynn Isabella, of the Darden Business School, University of Virginia. She is a regular contributor to IEDC's programs and wrote benchmark teaching cases on Lek Pharmaceuticals, milk producer Ljubljanske

Mlekarne, and Bobinac at Gorenje. These cases not only have "local and regional" appeal, notes Lynn, they fascinate students and managers studying at Darden who "also learn a tremendous amount about the struggle companies are facing in that part of the world."

Leadership and the Arts

"At the school, we were confronted with an innovating theme of Arts and Leadership," says an IEDC MBA graduate. "It is a daring concept, and brand, but also a theme that distinguishes this school from the mainstream. And there was a lot to learn. How many aspiring leaders have faced the opportunity to lead a choir and conduct the singers and their voices and try and turn it into something that makes sense? There was both fun and learning on that day and I think we all gained respect for artistic leadership."

Danica has had personal and pedagogical leanings to the arts throughout her life. Recall her early interests in theater, her storytelling at the Sorbonne, and her use of poetry and film in her teaching years at universities in Maribor and Ljubljana. Plus she married an artist, Arnold, who contributes to IEDC's arts and leadership program. The arts program at IEDC was initially an add-on to the MBA curricula and executive programs. One of its first artist-educators was Slovene Miha Pogačnik who started playing violin as a child of five and began performing a few years later. He recalls, "It blew my mind to have heard Henryk Szeryng at 14. From then on, all I wanted to do was to become a violinist," At 18, he went to study with master teachers at the Conservatory in Cologne, Germany and traveled to the U.S. on a Fulbright scholarship in the 1970s. There he participated in a program to teach handicapped adults the "art of listening." His career as a concert violinist transformed into one of societal engagement and Miha contributed to multicultural festivals in Amazonia, Tibet, Mongolia, Russia, Bosnia and Herzegovina, and Slovenia over the next two decades.

Like select others, Miha turned his attentions to "art and business" in the 1990s. "I wanted to take art out of the cultural ghetto and the ivory tower," he reports, "and move it to the centre of our society. The role of the arts is not to be the poor cousin of business....In contemporary society, artists shouldn't wait to be called, they must go into the territory and make in-roads... become co-authors and solution-providers of modern dilemmas." In saying so, he found a kindred spirit in Danica and soon he was contributing to programs at IEDC.

"Art can't just happen. It must make things happen," says entrepreneurial Miha. "By establishing a new relationship between the arts and business, bold visions can be considered and realized. The linear and rational must fuse with inspiration, beauty, and passion for change to be implemented." In 2005, he and Danica made things happen when IEDC sponsored a "five-module learning celebration built around the performance of 56 masterpieces of violin literature." Modules on the "ecology of the senses," "the heroic journey," "the feminine principle in leadership," and "arts- in-business" were introduced by violin compositions by Bach, Beethoven, Bartok, Mozart, Schubert, and Schumann and followed by lively discussion and applications to managing and to living beautifully.

Danish conductor Peter Hanke is another regular contributor to IEDC's arts and leadership program. His hands-on program has students and managers actually take the baton and conduct singers through a score. "It was a great experience to feel in practice the energetic connection between the leader and the 'followers," said one student. Another reported, "[the choir's] voices extended and lowered only by the slight movement of my hands and it was extraordinary...I could feel them depend on me." Listen to the way Danica and Ian describe its interior resonance: "As participants stood in front of the choir, experiencing a challenging leadership situation in the moment, they were able to see, hear, and *feel* themselves."

In the past few years, Haris (film studies) and Arnold (visual arts) have further embellished the arts and leadership program. Furthermore, the arts are being linked and connected into a full range of integrative learning experiences in company programs led by IEDC faculty, a subject taken up in the next chapter.

It needs to be said, however, that the arts-in-management program has had its challenging moments. "Artist's time," Danica growls, "is not the same as business time"—and there have been performances delayed or reshuffled because the performers haven't shown up on time. And not all corporate clients understand the importance of aesthetic experiences in leadership development programs; and not all of the MBAs see its relevance, either, but most come around.

For Niels van der Wel, an MBA student from the Netherlands, employed by a company that was acquired by a Slovenian firm, arts in management was initially a struggle. "My parents like art, classical music, and such things," Niels reported, "but these were not for me." Then, seeing films through Haris's eyes, taking up a baton to conduct an orchestra, and engaging other students who "see things differently," Niels became "angry with myself." "What have I missed?" He now tries to reflect on himself through art, explore his beliefs further through reading and film-going, and even talks to his parents about such things. "They are very surprised to see my new interests," he explained with a sheepish smile.

Riccardo Illy, Business Artist in Trieste

Who of the region's business leaders best exemplifies art in management? A case can be made for Riccardo Illy, Chairman of the Gruppo Illy, whose companies offer coffee, chocolates, tea, fruit jams, and now wine in over 140 countries around the world. Francesco Illy, his grandfather, of Hungarian origins, founded illycaffe as a joint venture in 1933 and produced coffee and chocolate. He operated a farm near Trieste in Istria, but after WWII lost it when Istria became part of Yugoslavia. Riccardo's father, Ernesto, transformed the small company into a modern one, controlled by the Illy family.

Riccardo started work in the family's coffee making firm in 1977. He reorganized the internal business structure and created the company's first marketing department to promote the illycaffe brand. He also wrote a book, *Dal Caffe all'Espresso* (From Coffeebeans to Espresso), that earned him the global moniker "missionary of espresso." (The photos for the book were made by his brother Francesco; brother Andrea today chairs illycaffe; mother Anna chairs the Ernesto Illy Foundation; and sister Anna is vice-chair of the Foundation and on the Boards of several companies in the Group.)

A click to the company's website reveals its deep connection to the arts: "illy has chosen art, literature and creativity as the languages to express its values and philosophy, for a complete coffee experience involving the eye and the mind. It all began in 1992, with the first collection of designer cups entitled 'Arts and Crafts,' which combined coffee with the aesthetics of the cup. Since then, illy has established a strong bond with the art world, constantly adding new encounters between the good and the beautiful."

The text goes on: "An ancient philosophical concept 'kalokagathia' teaches us that taste and beauty are inseparable: what is good cannot but be beautiful." It then lists artists involved in designing the cups—among them Michelangelo Pistoletto, Marina Abramovic, Sandro Chia, Julian Schnabel, Robert Rauschenberg, Jeff Koons, Joseph Kosuth, and James Rosenquist—and the company's research projects involving young artists in conjunction with organizations such as PS1 Contemporary Art Center in New York, the Central St. Martin's College in London, and the Fondazione Pistoletto in Rome.

Leading through Authenticity

For a first-hand experience of taste and beauty visit the company's headquarters in Trieste, a sleek, modernist structure set amidst graceful Italian churches and Austro-Hungarian offices and apartment buildings from earlier eras. Inside there is a stark white coffee bar with a barista brewing espressos; an exhibition of the designer cups and silver coffee tins, with the little red illy square; black-and-white images and a book by Brazilian photographer Sebastião Salgado that narrates the story of how the company works with coffee-growers in Brazil India, Ethiopia, and Guatemala toward more sustainable development; and if you're lucky, a chance to talk with the liquorer (cupper), who oversees the roasting of the coffee beans. In his office, Riccardo, trim, with a full head of silver-gray hair, offers a handshake and a smile.

In a paper on arts and leadership, Professor Nancy Adler writes, "Creating the next great thing demands constant innovation; it's a design task, not merely an analytical or administrative function. Historically, such creativity has been the primary competence of artists, not managers." That said, competitive strategies today emphasize beauty in product design and delivery as well as the more active and emotional engagement of customers. On these counts, Riccardo points to the many awards given to his company for its creative contributions and to those that illy gives to sustainable growers and espresso makers around the world. Plus there are a growing number of illy coffee shops, whose "authenticity" offers a high-end challenge to Starbucks, and the Universita Del Caffe, a two day course given by illy for wanna-be espresso baristas that extends the company's missionary coffee- brewing ambitions.

All of these art-in-management factors led Danica to reach out to Riccardo and invite him into the IEDC orbit. But she sought him as well for his statesmanship and for his deep interests in the social and economic development of the region.

Riccardo left the business ("an entrepreneur on loan to politics") to become Mayor of Trieste from 1993 to 2000; then in 2001 was elected an MP in the Italian Parliament; and in 2003 was elected President of the Regione Autonoma Friuli- Venezia Giulia, serving until April 2008. In this capacity, he associated himself with the expansion of the European Union and also worked on economic and trade development for the Adriatic—to foster cooperation between Italy, Slovenia, and Croatia—and, as he puts it, "to bury hatreds dating back to the rivalry during WWII."

In the classrooms at IEDC he talks with students about the "café experience," but in the President's forum and pan-European gatherings on campus he turns to continuing challenges in regional development. Now he is back full-time in the business world and a very active member of the IEDC Supervisory Board.

→ MAKING A BETTER WORLD

In its formative years at Brdo, IEDC hosted an international symposium on East-West business, featuring academics and leaders from business and government. Papers addressed industrial restructuring in socialist countries, privatization, exports and trade, the relevance of marketing and human resource management, and the experiences of CEE companies doing business in Western Europe. Chock full of graphs and tables, they told of bottlenecks, instability, old fashioned methods, and the like--the upshot being that insofar as competitiveness was concerned, "we've got a long way to go."

At its new location in Bled, 10 years later, IEDC hosted a conference on the competitiveness of companies where Slovenian President Kučan told a different story, "CEE companies are no longer from a completely different world." Among the achievements cited was the World Economic Forum's ranking of Slovenia as 31st on its scale of global country competitiveness. But while the President spoke proudly of progress he also spoke forcefully of challenges yet to be faced.

What should business, governments, societies do to respond to the 9/11 terrorist attack in New York City and to the "clash of civilizations" posed by political scientist Samuel P. Huntington, who predicted that people's cultural and religious identities would be the primary source of conflict in the post-Cold War world? What could they do in regard to growing gaps between rich and poor and threats to the planet due, in part, to the rise of global capitalism? "Anti-globalization movements as well as international terrorism," Kučan remarked, "are warning signals of the internal contradictions and conflicts in the modern world."

On these and other matters, he noted that Slovenia and CEE countries needed "joint deliberation" on cultural clashes and on "a perverted understanding of competitiveness which leads to production and provision of services with an ever- shrinking labor force and without sensitivity to nature, to life on the planet or its future, to humans, their dignity and rights." In anticipation of Slovenia joining the EU, which it would in 2004, he also told the audience that all of Europe needed to participate in this dialogue "in its own backyard."

Engaging with Society

IEDC's engagement locally, with the region, and with the larger CEE enlarged progressively from its founding into its leadership in CEEMAN. It took a new turn in 2002 when Erhard Busek was appointed coordinator of the Stability Pact for South Eastern Europe. The Stability Pact dates from 1998 and was formalized after the conflict in Kosovo as a vehicle to bring leaders from the Balkan states together with those from Europe, Japan, and North America to share ideas on democratization and to "build peace through economic development. "The Stability Pact established the Business Advisory Council for the region (BAC-SEE), and Danica was one of its two Slovene members. This Council would bring advice to governments of SEE on how to improve economic legislation, fight against corruption and so on. In contributing to its mission, IEDC developed programs in public administration for mid-level civil servants and higher-level managers from the region.

In 2003, a newly-formed European Leadership Centre (ELC) held its first meeting at IEDC-Bled under the leadership of its founders: Danica Purg, Derek Abell, and Professors Pierre Casse, Academic Dean, Berlin School for Creative Leadership, and Paul Claudel, IAE University, Aix-en-Provence, France (all of whom teach at IEDC). To introduce the program, Danica asked these orienting questions: "What does good European leadership mean? How is what makes a good leader now different from 10 years ago, and how will it be different in 10 years' time? What conclusions can we draw from current European leadership? What recommendations can we give to current and future leaders in Europe and in the world?"

At this first conference, Abell spoke about "leadership beyond the bottom line." Jonathan Gosling addressed the need for a "worldly mindset." He said, "The princess Europa was once seduced by Zeus in the form of a bull and carried away over the seas to Greece. She fell in love with the Greek way of doing things, and particularly with the notion that the highest human virtue was that of deliberation: trying to make judgments between competing values." This model he preferred to that of Britannia who "tried to rule the waves, to control even the winds and currents of the economy in her imperial interests."

Casse, summing up the proceedings, noted, "Our first conclusion is that we, Europeans, are too obedient and that breaking rules is always a positive thing. We came up with the idea that we should not wait for some kind of common, unified vision; we must force the emergence of such a vision." The ELC has been doing so ever since, meeting annually, addressing timely academic and practical pan- European leadership issues, and engaging close to 200 business, government, NGO and media leaders from 22 countries.

As for other types of engagement, IEDC has also helped its neighbors to throw a good party. In honor of Slovenia's admission to the European Union, IEDC hosted a 2004 conference: Bled to Europe, Europe to Bled. To introduce it, a gala performance was put on by Haris Pašović that featured a famous opera singer singing the EU and Slovenian anthems on Bled Lake, accompanied by a trumpet player. For its 20th anniversary celebration, Slovene composer Vinko Globokar had a symphony traverse Lake Bled on boats, with opera singers on the shoreline, and trumpets blowing from the hilltop castle. The rehearsal was superb, but the performance was met by pouring rain. Still, "the show must go on," and it did–to rave reviews.

Arts and Leadership = Creativity

The arts and leadership thrust gained momentum at IEDC the past five years and moved into the mainstream curriculum. Take Haris Pašović whose interests in management were piqued by the program with BAE Systems in Sarajevo: he went on to study with Jonathan Gosling in the U.K. and immersed himself in "critical management" studies. "It was very instructive, but neither sufficient nor courageous enough for my interests," he reported. Now he teaches an IEDC module using films to highlight the dynamic aspects of leadership. One film, *1492: Conquest of Paradise,* raises thoughtful questions about the leadership of Christopher Columbus: How courageous do you have to be as a leader to realize your vision? How do you answer doubters and meet the material, psychological, and metaphysical needs of your followers? And, more provocatively, was Columbus a hero for journeying to the New World or instead a conqueror serving royal interests in Spain?

Arnold Walravens, in turn, has introduced a module on the visual arts—using paintings as a mirror for students. He starts the class showing one of his own paintings—"You see I am not an artist!"—to illustrate how he uses painting for reflection. Next he presents a tableau of ideas expressed through the history of art, taking students through Greco-Roman, realistic, romantic, and abstract expressionist artwork. Surprisingly, he says, both the MBAs and managers identify most with romantic paintings (rather than realistic ones that would seem to suit their business interests). Later he takes the class on a virtual tour around the school to see its artwork. "Which one would you take home with you?" he asks. Most favor artworks that match their stylistic preferences.

These aesthetic experiences open up conversation and reflection. Managers understand how to think, but can they truly see the world within and around themselves? The class reflects on the "observing" mind. Participants had favored artworks that match their preferred style. Arnold challenges them: How about seeking diversity? What is your comfort with people that are different from you? In addition, many students bring their own paintings, pictures, and drawings to class. This leads to fuller disclosure of "who I am and what moves me" and to dialogue about how to express creativity in everyday life and work.

The latest addition to the arts and leadership faculty is Canadian Ian Sutherland, a pianist with a Ph.D. in sociology and philosophy, recruited by Danica, who arrived at IEDC in January, 2011. "I got a call from her when she was at the Academy of Management meetings in Montreal," he reports, "took a four-hour flight, changed clothes fast, and we talked for some hours. Then she said come with me to Dubrovnik where we can together do a session on creativity for managers of Erste Group." Ian brings an academic's interest and concert performer's talent to art and leadership. On the scholarly side, Ian joined Danica to write about the many parallels between music making and managing and he teamed with Italian Luca Gatti, another IEDC faculty, to explore how aesthetic sensibilities can enrich business strategy.

In the classroom, he aims for participants to get a "deeper grounding in current experience." Music, for example, "fills the space;" painting provides a "singular focus;" and "scenic parameters challenge assumptions about what's going on." All of this stimulates reflection and "sense making." In their group discussions, he goes on, "People have to situate the experience. What's happening to me? Where are you?"

To illustrate his methods, Ian reports in his essay in this volume how in one program, managers watched and listened to John Cage's composition 4 '33" ("Four minut thirty-three seconds") via YouTube. Designed for any combination of instruments, the piece unfolds in three movements, each scored, where the only requirement is that the musicians do not play their instruments. The result is 4 '33" of silence. Midway through, Danica, who was unfamiliar with the work, nudged Ian that "it is not playing." Afterwards, the managers, having been taken "out of their comfort zone" engaged in lively conversation about how going-in assumptions shape their view of things. Ian recorded their observations on flip charts and pressed them for the implications in practice.

Bringing Creativity into Business Education

In an address on arts and leadership, Danica put its appeal in business education into this perspective: "Business schools are at a crossroads. They are shifting from a reliance on analytical models and statistics to developing leadership skills of self-awareness and self-reflection. They are teaching a global mindset and an understanding of the roles and responsibilities of business as well as the limitations of existing business models and markets."

She went on to cite a study by Nigel Andrews and Laura D'Andrea Tyson who surveyed the top 100 employers in the U.K. about why only a third of them were hiring MBAs from the London Business School. They also interviewed some 100 chief executive officers of big companies in North America, Asia, South America, and the Middle East, and asked them if business schools provided what the businesses needed.

The study produced a list of qualities that chief executives desired from a recruit. The list did not include any functional or technical knowledge—the core subjects of the MBA curricula. Instead, as Danica summarizes it, the CEOs wanted "more thoughtful, more aware, more sensitive, more flexible, and more adaptive managers capable of being molded and developed into global executives."

There is today a global arts-in-management community of over 400 scholars, practitioners, and artists called AACORN (Arts, Aesthetics, Creativity, and Organization Research Network). IEDC has been at the forefront of this movement—taking a global leadership role. Nancy Adler, a professor, painter, and leading advocate of linking arts to business, has been to IEDC many times. On her first visit she was to join in a performance with violinist Miha Pogačnik: the plan was for Miha to play and Nancy to paint impressions of the music. Well, Miha was waylaid ("to be polite" says Nancy) and their duet became a solo of painting and talking. She continues to lecture, perform, and engage with IEDC students and managers on arts and leadership.

Another visiting ambassador was Edgar Schein, MIT professor emeritus and scholar of corporate culture who loves to draw. He came to IEDC for a program on the future of human resource management where he gave a spell-binding interview on art. Reflecting on his visit, Danica recalls him saying: "Art is making us feel more, hear more, and see more; it is putting us in touch with our creative self." What these musicians, painters, film-makers, and composers do at IEDC is to highlight the aesthetic, sensory-emotional, non-rational aspects of human experience to help future managers and leaders come to deeper understandings of themselves and their organizations, of those with whom they work and serve, and of the wider world. When listening to Miles Davis's seminal jazz album *Kind of Blue* or conducting a choir, they develop skills of awareness, sensitivity, and empathy; they question basic assumptions about business and the world of work; and they enter into the realm of creative expression. Through the works of artists, they learn to see beyond the traditional, conventional, and ordinary and to realize more of their own creative potential and its possibilities.

Bringing Creativity into Business Practice

Businesses, too, are waking up to the need for more creativity. From 1985 to 2005, firms in the U.S. and Western Europe were focused on what is euphemistically called "value extraction"—reducing their ranks, restructuring, outsourcing, and offshoring--doing everything they could to cut costs in light of competition from China and the Asia-Pacific. Meanwhile, their rates of growth declined. Attentions then necessarily returned to "value creation"—innovation, new product and service offerings, and new business models. This, leading firms understood, would require unlocking the creative talent latent in their workforces and management.

Eureko, the largest insurance provider in the Netherlands, found one key to prepare their managers for this future in a one-week seminar on "Leading Change, Identity and Values." As Danica describes it "We took the managers to Bosnia and Herzegovina, where people have a problem with identity. We met with artists who told us how they managed risk during the war, with an architect who talked about architecture as expression of identity, and we had discussions with former prime ministers who told us how they were coping with the changes. I can tell you that during those seven days I saw what we should all aim for in management education: reflection and transformation."

Eureko's core values speak to empathizing with customers, to innovating in the market, and to delivering on their brand's promise. In Sarajevo, they walked though cobbled streets and past mass graveyards, clambered through the tunnel where help came into and refugees fled from the city; they talked later in Bled about global issues affecting the insurance industry; and finished the program with Miha Pogačnik's "decomposition" of music. Taken together, these activities were woven into a transformative experience for the Eureko team.

A central feature in this program was "story-telling." After hearing the leadership stories of politicians, for instance, Eureko's managers shared their own leadership stories–the ups-and-downs and lessons learned. Psychologist Howard Gardner underscores the relevance of this kind of exercise for executive development in his emphasis on "identity stories" as a means of connecting leaders and followers: "Identity stories have their roots in the personal experiences of the leader in the course of his (or her) own development. But it is characteristic of the effective leader that this story can be transplanted to a larger canvas–that makes sense not only to members of his family and close circle, but to increasingly larger entities...."

After sharing leadership stories, the Eureko team began listing the personal implications: "Sense of urgency; Dare to be more vulnerable; It all starts with ourselves." They then transplanted these themes to an action agenda for their enterprise: "Don't wait for the Supervisory Board--We create Change, Understand strategic risks–Develop our own process; Frame the Future–Listen to our own narrative." This inspired the managers to develop specific strategies for their business and emboldened them to grow their top line.

In sum, art and artistic experiences can open people's minds and eyes, shock and provoke them, and stimulate and inspire. They can also be a source of innovation and renewal for business. My own action studies have examined how managers use "performativity" to awaken their companies to change, inspire and mobilize support, and give direction and meaning to new strategies and undertakings. This puts them into the role of a director, rather than a manager, in staging events, and transforms change plans into a script, with scenes, roles, and dramaturgy lending both a heroic and playful aspect to the action. Tex Gunning, then a senior executive with Unilever, successfully orchestrated the rescue of a failing business in the Netherlands in the 1990s with this approach and brought it to double-digit growth. He later built the company's foods business in Asia by leading 250-plus executives through a series of artful and consciousness-raising experiences throughout the Asia-Pacific region.

Expanding IEDC's Mission and Reach

In his 2001 address, President Kučan spoke of larger ambitions and contributions for businesses in his country and the CEE, citing the Union Nation's Millennium Development Goals that include laudatory aims such as halving extreme poverty and hunger around the globe, reducing infant mortality by two-thirds, achieving universal primary education, empowering women, and creating global partnerships for development. On this point, Peter Kraljič, next on the dais, challenged his compatriots and colleagues that "even small countries need global leaders."

Taking up this challenge in 2006, IEDC's 20th anniversary celebration and the book published on the occasion were themed "Leadership for a Better World." The school--as an "agent of change"--was expanding its mission. Janez Drnovšek, elected Slovenia's president in 2002, wrote in his contribution about the importance of strategy "based on sustainable development." Pedro Nueno argued for a new generation of corporate social responsibility. Danica and Arnold stressed the importance of the United Nation's Global Compact (UNGC) that brings companies together with UN agencies, governments, and civil society to support and advance universal principles of responsible business conduct concerning, for example, human rights, labor, environmental responsibility, and anti-corruption.

"Every single social and global issue of our day is a business opportunity in disguise." Peter Drucker discussed this idea with Professor David Cooperrider, of Case Western Reserve University in Cleveland, in a conversation about corporate social responsibility versus profits. Dave was about to launch a Center for Business as an Agent of World Benefit (BAWB) which includes Danica on its advisory board. At the inaugural BAWB conference, co-sponsored by Case, the Academy of Management (AOM), and United Nations Global Compact, hundreds of managers, scholars, and students in attendance listened to "doing well by doing good" presentations by the CEOs of Unilever, Lafarge, and Fairchild mining, debated the synergies and conflicts between "profits" and "principles," and heard from academic leaders on what all this innovation and clamor might mean for management education and business leadership. It is at this conference that Danica and I first met.

Nadya Zhexembayeva, then a Ph.D. student at Case and BAWB conference organizer, had been pondering these matters in the context of CEE countries for some time. In a blog entry of that era she noted, "The West is trying to teach East about social responsibility--while the East has just converted to the capitalist agenda and is ditching its social agenda"; she also pointed her finger at the International Monetary Fund's inattention to social welfare and the environment. Dave's entry challenged her, "So the fundamental institutions that really drive the world economy haven't really changed in their conceptions of the role of business in society?" Nadya replied that "the politics of development still push it in that traditional direction," but added "consumers are driving a different definition of development, toward more sustainability."

A colleague retorted, "In Croatia consumers have no power--they can't even return things at the store. The whole value system in Croatia is messed up--showing off bankrupts people who go out and spend money to drive a BMW, yet live in poverty. This is the problem with the traditional way of defining development, where development is materialism." The session concluded with Nadya raising this big question in capital letters: HOW CAN BUSINESS DEVELOP IN MY HOME COUNTRY IN A POSITIVE WAY?

Nadya joined the IEDC faculty in 2007, the same year that the Slovene chapter of the UN Global Compact was established, based at IEDC with 53 member organizations and Danica as its president and Nadya named its vice-president. The next year Queen Elizabeth II and The Duke of Edinburgh joined them in a conference on "Sustainable Development for National Competitiveness" organized by the UNGC Slovenia, IEDC, and UK Trade & Investment. The conference featured best sustainable business practices from Slovenian and U.K. companies, including presentations by Janez Škrabec, Tatjana Fink, Jon Pender, of GlaxoSmithKline, and Žiga Debeljak, of the Mercator Group.

Challenge:Future

Nadya has become a recognized authority on sustainability with the publication of her book *Embedded Sustainability: The Next Big Competitive Advantage* (co-authored with Chris Laszlo) and is its champion in the IEDC classroom. She and Danica have joined forces with colleague Olga Veligurska from CEEMAN and with Andreja Kodrin from Third Millennium Knowledge who is founder and president of Challenge: Future (C:F) to launch a project for youth who "want to make a better world." C:F is the world's largest youth collaborative contest that uses web 2.0 technologies to create a virtual forum where students age 18 through 30 can submit innovations to address the world's leading social and environmental challenges.

IEDC hosted the 2010 Challenge: Future Summit in Bled that featured peer discussions and lectures from experts in different fields. The leading topic was sustainable development: climatologist Lučka Kajfež Bogataj presented evidence about how economic development is putting the planet under threat and Nadya talked about how for-profit businesses can be a great source of sustainable innovation. The highlight was the introduction of the student finalists in the competition.

The 2010 winners, Yen Ching Liew and Chen Sin Tan from Singapore, won the grand award of €20,000 for their proposal to redesign the doors on subway trains. The two explained in a blog addressed to future contestants: "In a highly populated, rapidly developing country like Singapore, the efficiency of the public transport system is one of the key factors towards the development of the country....A few years back, when we were riding the Metro, we experienced a saturated train capacity problem --squeezed in and out of the train during rush hour causes a lot of delay in the travelling time of commuters. By that time, both of us were so frustrated about it and we had a wild thought of having the entire stretch of the side wall of the metro train be transformed into a door that opened upwards rapidly so that the commuters can alight and board the train more easily...."

Their proposal, Nmetro, could reduce the passengers travel time by 25 percent, increase train network capacity by 50 percent, and reduce the number of trains required for a system by 25 percent. According to analysts, this new metro design can save money for government as well as the taxpayers, and reduce the raw material and energy required for a greener metro design.

The winning team's blog added, "We love the way C:F organized the competition, the way that they gather talents and how they let us develop the solutions and interact among each other, that's what made us jump in, similarly this is also the reason that made us so supportive of this competition after the event :)"

Hidden Champions

IEDC's current emphasis on innovation extends well beyond the classroom, the UNGC Slovenia, and mobilizing youth. For instance, faculty member Melita Rant is leading a group of colleagues in CEEMAN schools to identify "hidden champions" among small- and mid-size businesses in CEE countries. Among the winners found so far include a Latvian firm that manufactures wind tunnels, a Croatian firm leading with mining technology, and a Slovene enterprise that has developed the lightest plane in the world.

Why is research like this worthwhile? Often business innovations come not from the big firms or start-ups, but from mid-size enterprises that develop products at a technological edge and that secure market leadership based on quality, rather than cost, and superior customer service. Many midsize companies in the CEE region face a choice on how to grow: by winning in a market or by becoming a small part of a multinational company's supply chain. The latter option, while surely a challenge, can become "soulless" over time, focusing management on incremental process improvements. The champions that Melita and her team are studying have bigger ambitions but need a new generation of leaders and managers to continue innovating and to diversify. The knowledge gained by this research, to be shared in writings and at conferences, could be a treasure trove. There are currently about 120 innovative companies from 22 countries that are being researched.

Sandi Češko, Commercial and Social Entrepreneur

On matters of innovation and sustainability, a very visible champion in Slovenia is Sandi Češko, Executive Chairman, Studio Moderna Group. Sandi started in 1992 as an electronics retailer and today runs the leading online, multichannel retailer in 21 countries in Central and Eastern Europe. Why did he become an entrepreneur? "For four years following my graduation from the local university in political science, I served in a youth leadership position, and although there were many positive changes and an optimism in the air in the late 1980s, I became disillusioned because as part of the political sphere we were not encouraged to actually accomplish anything and it was the pretenders that were rewarded. I was attracted to direct marketing to be relatively free of 'non-market' influences."

He started with a computing business where "we unlocked Japanese computers for bar code printers to be able to install local characters on time for our buyer." While the Japanese manufacturers were initially outraged at this, they asked him to provide this service also for many other languages.

In 1991 his friend Branimir Brkljač introduced him to Kosmodisk, an anatomically designed belt to address back pain. He agreed with his wife that she would start to sell Kosmodisk, while he would stay dedicated to his high tech business. But soon he realized that his wife, Livija Dolanc, was more successful growing her business, so he asked himself: "Why is she making more money than me?" He joined with her and back pain relief was their first product sold through DRTV (Direct Response Television).

Today Studio Moderna employs 5000 people and offers a wide range of products curated specifically for CEE consumers, including its own proprietary brands and others' products. "Our IT system allows us to create close to 100 virtual warehouses (for each country and for every distribution channel) and each country is able to view their orders and where products are physically located. Each channel manager can see the status of all of the products in his or her channel. So managers who need product can communicate their needs to others in the system, and they can negotiate." Sandi goes on to say, "We created our systems from scratch and this is a big competitive advantage for us. Our competitors have huge SAP or Oracle applications which take months to change. Our system allows us to scale efficiently." Today all business processes in the company are digitalized and everybody responsible for sales can check his or her result or ROI on a daily basis. Around 600 managers are using IT systems on a daily basis to make decisions.

Studio Moderna's success caught the eye of Daniel Isenberg, Professor of Management Practice and founding executive director of the Babson Entrepreneurship Ecosystem Project, who described Sandi as a "minnovator." In his blog for the *Harvard Business Review*, Isenberg writes, "In reality, the vast majority of real-life entrepreneurs around the world aren't innovators. They're minnovators–mixing small parts of novelty and creativity with huge helpings of flexibility, scrappiness and a generous portion of hard-driving execution." He goes on to say, "When Češko saw the large TV shopping companies from the U.S. fail in Eastern Europe, he took their strategy of outsourcing the critical functions–infomercial creation, call centers, delivery, payment–to third parties and stood it on its head: Češko minnovated by insourcing those functions, bringing them in-house so that he could achieve an unprecedented level of service, and in doing so, he won Eastern European consumers' trust in a very untrusting market. "

Leadership Lessons

Sandi boasts today that he has no personal assistant and hardly any administrators in his company. Instead everyone in his company has a PDA, interacts on line, and updates financial records electronically 24/7. How has IEDC helped him and his company to succeed in this fast-past, digitized environment? Sandi thinks a minute and then credits the school with giving him, and many of his employees who attend school programs, "confidence in everyday experiments." At IEDC, he says, you find "creativity" and "out of the box thinking" to be staples in the curricula and classroom.

He especially credits the atmosphere and values of the school for shaping his managerial style. "I can challenge people; people can challenge me; there's give- and-take without worry "what does the boss think." "If we have the toughest laboratory inside the company, then we are more likely to survive the pressure of the market outside. People, especially in Europe, don't want to challenge others face to face because they take criticism personally. Here I encourage innovative thinking and brainstorming, but also request colleagues to try and shoot down new ideas in our meetings."

A tour of the Studio Moderna headquarters takes you from spartan offices to a showroom of mattresses to an open office space filled with telemarketers and computers to a hallway filled with bicycles that appear to be folded in half. These are lightweight "Bigfish" bikes that can be folded in seconds with no screwing action or tools. Their ergonomics and dimensions are the same as full-sized bikes, and the bikes provide, so the advertising says, "a comfortable ride, while the 16in wheels give an added 'zip' for tight city streets."

The bikes were a big hit at the Clinton Global Initiative (CGI) Annual Meeting in New York in 2010 where they were pitched as an environmentally-conscious way to help mass transit commuters to get to-and-from transit stations. At the CGI, Bigfish announced two green demonstration projects in the U.S.: 1) participation in 15 'mobility hubs' in the greater Los Angeles area, and 2) placement of the bikes in businesses located in suburban LA where they could contribute to a company's sustainable commuting efforts. Sandi points proudly to a picture of Bill Clinton and himself looking over a Bigfish bike at the CGI meeting.

Reflecting on the 2010 CGI meeting, Sandi said it was "new, exciting, and no place for passengers." Motivated by this experience, he sponsored a conference in 2011 at IEDC Bled titled, "Building a European Network of Corporate Social Responsibility & Philanthropy, with special participation of the Clinton Global Initiative."

IEDC and the Clinton Global Initiative

Sandi Češko welcomed 90 business leaders, philanthropists, social entrepreneurs and heads of public organizations from eighteen countries to the conference on May 16, 2011 at IEDC. "The purpose of CGI is not to collect cash," he said, "but to focus on ideas and commitments to concrete actions, directed towards positive change." He went on to describe his own company's investments in a Balkan Child and Youth Foundation and its program in Moldova, where unemployment is running at 60 percent. So far the program has put 900 youth into training programs, 350 into business internships, and 259 into paying jobs.

In an interview he explained his motivations, "We want to be integrated into the community around us and to help to change it for the better. This is our responsibility to those who can't help themselves and to all of us who believe in a better world."

Next up, former U.S. President Bill Clinton appeared in a video and reported that CGI members have made nearly 2000 commitments valued at $63 billion USD, which have already improved more than 300 million lives in 180 countries. These include investments in mobile phones to reduce the "digital divide," in micro-lending and insurance, in sustainable agriculture, and in tackling counterfeit drugs. Robert S. Harrison, the former Goldman Sachs banker turned CEO of the CGI, added that some 350 of these initiatives are complete and that 37 have stalled. The delegates present were then challenged for ideas on how to pick up the pace, scale the impact, and keep things moving forward despite tough economic times.

IEDC was well represented on panels by its faculty and two of its alumni. On the more academic side of things, Violeta Bulc, an IEDC graduate, spoke on "Social Awareness for the New Millennium." "Evolution revolves and leaves evidence of its passing. We can see its effects everywhere: in our relationships with life, nature, universe, and ourselves. Consequently it changes the way we do business, how we act as integrated community members, as consumers, and as co-creators of the present time. Social entrepreneurship, sustainable local supply chains, environmental consciousness, awareness of global interconnectedness and mutual dependencies are just a few signals about a transformation that is happening in our society....Are we on a verge of a new impulse for value creation, of a new set of values, new consciousness?"

In her studies at IEDC, Violeta had been a "challenge" for some of the faculty. Nenad, for example, "didn't know what to do with her," but Arnold served as her advisor and found her a "gem." Bright, curious, she became a devotee of the "new science of leadership," which draws its ideas on leading from chaos theory, quantum physics, and the study of complex, adaptive systems and connects them to theories on the evolution of human consciousness and its trajectory toward a better future.
This line of theorizing about leadership extends beyond positive psychology and into the realm of what some describe as the "spiritual sciences" and others as "new age" thinking. While this is not the usual stuff of management school education, it has informed the outlooks of many practitioners and academics who follow the work of Otto Scharmer (who lectured at IEDC), Peter Senge, Joe Jaworski, and other learning organization theorists who have made "presencing" a new methodology for thinking about and realizing a better future. The emphasis is on "inner knowing" in this model and from that deep source gaining new perspective on the world. Central is the idea that all of life is connected via "fields" of consciousness. The methodology has groups of people co-sense their inner life and the world around them, use their collective intelligence and will to connect with emerging forces, co-create new actions, and co-evolve with transformation in a field that has been influenced by their own doings.

Now all of this may sound brilliant or like quackery, depending on your understandings and point of view, but many in the audience, especially the young people, eagerly took notes as Violeta described companies as "living organisms," shared examples of new business models based on co-evolution, and challenged attendees "to develop personally one's emotional and spiritual world (so that) we understand the subtle differences in value systems between the different nations." She added that the "ability to transition between systems of values is one of the key elements of good co-creation."

Social Entrepreneur

Gazmend Haxhia, an Albanian who attended two programs at IEDC, contributes to many of its programs today, and was named a Young Global Leader in 2008 by the Davos Economic Forum jury. He provided the forum with a somewhat more down-to-earth story of co-creation by sharing his experiences at POLIS University that he established in Tirana, Albania, where students study architecture, planning, and urban management. Gazmend, a lifelong mover-and-shaker, set up a program that brings in 400 students, "one-half from the streets of Tirana," to get an education in urban planning to "rebuild the nation."

Born in Tirana in 1968, he was told by his parents and two elder sisters that the "sky is the limit if we try and work hard and do it honestly." He graduated from the local university and attended Columbia University in New York, from which he holds a Master's degree in International Affairs. Returning to Albania, he was encouraged to go into political leadership. Instead, he laughs, "I have nine business cards. When my wife saw the card from Polis University, she cried, 'Not another one!'"

When asked to characterize his school, Gazmend said it was a "social innovation." The POLIS website proclaims: "In Albania there is a contrasting environment which stands between realism and surrealism, between communism and capitalism, between standard architecture and temptations towards the most extreme creativity....While for many this is only a 'chaos,' POLIS believes in the positive energy that the city and the entire society are generating....We try to formalize a new way of thinking about architecture and to establish the 'new profession' of urban planner, so much needed in the Albanian reality."

Reflecting on his entrepreneurial life–as businessman, educator, political advisor, social activist, and more–Gazmend touches on many of the themes emphasized at IEDC. He writes, "Entrepreneurship is a social phenomenon, and the process of how one becomes (an entrepreneur) is socially embedded. This progress is more about shaping and focusing business ideas and the first stages of the entrepreneurial process revolve around the ambiguity of 'who am I'?"

"Albanian entrepreneurs clearly understand that entering the entrepreneurship game is about making money; but it is also about making a mark. The new generation is endlessly better educated and informed than their predecessors and shamelessly entrepreneurial. For many, a dull corporate existence is not an option. They want more than just a check at the end of the month... many want meaning and purpose as well. Many of them want to change the world, to follow their star, taking the future in their own hands. For a growing number of young people, creating a business has become a calling, a vocation. It is a mission in itself. They think they are offered the opportunity not just to make money but to make history in their own way in their own clusters and communities."

"Nowadays, companies understand they exist in a social context. In an increasing number of cases they understand that consumers and customers are prepared to put their wallets where their principles are. Consumers nowadays are more informed, concerned and aware about issues that directly affect their health and social well-being. A case in point is the expiry date of goods which can no longer be manipulated like before, or product labeling that now needs to be in Albanian. Knowing that reality has made entrepreneurs tailor their approach accordingly, a sure sign that the rules of business are changing. The case today is that consumer interest in ethical issues is moving the goalposts for companies."

Based on the foregoing, it is not surprising that many young people in the audience thrust their business cards into Gazmend's hands as he struggled to choose which of his business cards to give to them in return. As we walked together out of the CGI meeting, Gazmend reflected warmly on his countryman and mentor, Ichak Adizes, "who is like a brother to me." He was heading off to another multisector, multiparty gathering in the region, flying with Derek Abell. "Small world," he remarked.

→ POSTSCRIPT

Ichak Adizes was born October 22, 1937 in Skopje, the capital of Macedonia. As he records it, "My family was the descendants of the Jews that were expelled from Spain in 1492 for refusing to convert to Christianity during the time of the Inquisition. From Spain the family escaped to Verona, Italy where they took the name of the river Adige for their family name. In the beginning of the 16th century they settled in Macedonia."

During WWII, all of the Jews in Macedonia, over 7000, were herded into concentration camps by Bulgarian fascists and nearly all, including his extended family, died in the ovens of Treblinka. Ichak and his parents were spared because his father had succeeded, based on the family's lineage, to secure a Spanish passport. "We escaped to Albania aided by smugglers whom we bribed. We pretended to be Muslims from Bosnia, escaping a blood revenge. My father was aware of a Muslim cultural tradition which he knew would assist us in hiding....Until the end of the war we survived because my dad pretended to be a medical doctor. Using his wits and a basic knowledge of hygiene he helped many people. In return for this we received food."

After the war, the family moved to Israel where Ichak served in the army and completed his undergraduate degree. In 1963, he went to the U.S. to earn a Ph.D. in business from Columbia, then joined the faculty of UCLA, and later established the Adizes Institute, a consulting firm advising on business growth and development. He has long been a friend of Danica, leads programs regularly at IEDC, and was awarded an honorary doctorate in 2007 at the campus.

Getting to Prime

Ichak was one the earliest and most influential theorists to identify stages in the growth of an enterprise. In generic formulation, the stages involve a creative start-up, then development of infrastructure and capacities to manage greater responsibilities, and then the ongoing struggle to balance competing tendencies toward stability versus change, adaptation versus innovation, and integration versus differentiation through to maturity.

In Adizes' model, the central challenge for managers is getting their companies to "Prime"—an optimal point where the organization finally achieves a balance between control and flexibility. What are the characteristics of an organization in Prime? Some of them include:

- The organization is guided by the vision of its reason for being. There is a clear purpose and people know what they will do, and will not do, "they walk their talk."
- The company operates in a focused, energized and predictable manner.
- Stretch goals are set, aligned, and consistently achieved.
- There is an enterprise-wide focus on customers and earning their long-term satisfaction.
- Priorities are clear. The organization knows what to do, and what not to do.
- The entrepreneurial spirit is fully institutionalized. This creativity repeatedly produces controlled, profitable innovation.
- Organizational structures work well. Opposing forces are balanced.
- The governance process is institutionalized. People know and understand where and how decisions are made.
- People enjoy working at the company.
- Prime companies work hard to adapt to changes in markets and technology so that they can gain share from weaker competitors. They embrace change.

IEDC's Supervisory Board has held the management school to account annually on these kinds of criteria. Its 2006 review reported good progress on increasing the percentage on non-Slovenian participants in IEDC programs—from 60 percent to 70 percent from 2001 to 2006. Further efforts on this objective increased non- Slovenian participation to 80 percent in 2010.

By comparison, the 2006 review found that IEDC could do more to activate its alumni network. Over the next five years, alumni clubs in 12 countries would grow, host seminars and conferences, recruit students, and sponsor annual events: a film festival in Bosnia, sailing regatta in Croatia, and rowing races in Slovenia at Bled. And, as for rowing races, IEDC co-hosted the BMW Eco Regatta held on Lake Bled in May, 2011. With IT specialist Gregor Repe rowing madly alongside two alumni and a professional, and Danica as coxswain, the IEDC team won its first heat but faded in the semi-finals. Apart from supporting charities through the competition, the regatta aimed to showcase the "greening" of business in Slovenia. IEDC's in-house Green Team hosted a fully-recyclable luncheon for contestants.

Overall, the Supervisory Board has given IEDC good marks on key elements of vision, customer-focus, staff motivation and innovations in leadership development, and internationalization. The results attest to achievement: School revenue increased over 225 percent from 2000 to 2010, despite the economic recession that still lingers, and over the ten years the cumulative number of students/participants in IEDC programs increased by nearly 250 percent. All of this suggests that IEDC has reached or is nearing a Prime point in its life cycle.

In life cycle models of organizational growth, however, the founder seldom leads his or her company to Prime. Because they are typically too risk-oriented, demanding, and ego-centric, founders of successful organization are often pushed out of operational roles--after 10 to 15 years tops–and more professional managers are put in place to provide the structure and direction necessary for further growth. How does this finding apply to IEDC?

Strategy as Stretch

Mariola Ciszewska-Mlinarič, of Kozminski University (CEEMAN school member in Poland), believes she has found the key to Danica's successful leadership of IEDC to

Prime. In a paper on "Strategy as Fit or Stretch? Implications for International Entrepreneurship," presented at an international conference, she contends that IEDC has continually "stretched" in its ambitions, boundaries, and reach. The backdrop: One segment of the business strategy literature emphasizes the importance of an organization achieving a "fit" with its environment. This fit equates to adaptation and ensures profits. Another school of thought favors aggressive moves to stay ahead of developments in a firm's environment. This is expressed as foresight by Gary Hamel and C. K Prahalad in *Competing for the Future* and often takes form as a BHAG (Big, Hairy, Audacious Goal) according to Jerry Porras and Jim Collins in *Built to Last*.

In Mariola's analysis, Danica's insistence on "only the best" and her ambitions to "be one of the best business schools in Europe" constitute a BHAG. Clearly, she points out, this didn't "fit" the prevailing ethos and management education market in Yugoslavia in 1986. On the contrary, she asserts, "it was a purposeful creation of misfit." Foresight and the purposeful creation of misfit were also behind the launch of CEEMAN, the IEDC President's MBA, the European Leadership Centre, and the Arts and Leadership program in ensuing years. Adding to this, Mariola writes, "Although IEDC achievements are notable, there is no room for self-complacency;" and then quotes Danica as saying, "We are happy but never satisfied. We have still unused potential. Now in our MBA Class we have representatives from 15 countries, in the future we would like to have 30, 40!"

Managers who adopt the stretch philosophy—setting impossible-to-reach goals and leading their companies to an uncertain and risky future—claim that it frees-up creative imagination and competitive instincts in their companies. It requires continuous re-invention. She quotes Danica again on how this process worked at IEDC: "In the past we were focused on developing knowledge for leaders, today we want to develop responsible leaders, responsible not only for the organization and employees, but also for the society at large."

There are of course leaders and organizations that set ambitious visions and goals that reduce to sloganeering: *Be the Industry Leader, #1 or #2 in Our Markets,* and so on. The successful ones detail that vision to show how and why to move from current reality to a desired future and infuse it with values so that people want to go there. Over the past 25 years, IEDC has followed a path to Prime that took new turns, but in so doing, it continually refreshed its guiding mission and chose its new directions wisely.

What Is Next?

In his address at IEDC in 2009, Adizes stressed another critical element for organizations at Prime: "You have to maintain commitment beyond the founder." My interviews with Supervisory Board members, staff, and visiting and local faculty all concluded with a question about "what's next" for IEDC. Almost all said that the school should continue to globalize, continue to innovate in arts and leadership, and continue to operate as an agent of change. But all said, too, that they worry about what will happen when Danica retires.

Speaking to this, Danica laughs that everyone at the school has been "poisoned" with her emphasis on quality and carries it in their bloodstream. She says, "In the past, when I was away for a couple of weeks, I could expect all sorts of problems at the school. Now, however, my staff has been so infused with this philosophy of challenge and innovation that they hardly need to be supervised. Instead of coming back from my travels to find problems, I come back to requests for meetings: everybody wants me to see all that they have been doing while I was away."

She goes on, "The philosophy of excellence, of continuously creating, is so inculcated that on their own staff members will not allow for any concessions to be made to it. In fact, regularly, they even surpass me in their striving for perfection...This has allowed me to withdraw from the day-to-day management of operations and I consider this another success in the development of our institution."

Nevertheless, there is concern that it may be hard to retain current IEDC faculty, now well-known globally, should bigger schools offering larger salaries recruit them. Jim Ellert frets that the school's visiting faculty is "getting grayer," and has not yet been supplemented by world-class professors in their 30s and 40s. "Their schools don't want them to go to Bled," he says, "IEDC has become a formidable competitor!" Another faculty worries that there is not a sufficient leadership "team" at IEDC.

All of these concerns will be on the agenda of the Supervisory and Academic Boards of IEDC in the near term and are also on Danica's mind. Given the importance of stretch in shaping the school's vision and achievements, looking further out it seems likely that IEDC will have to reinvent itself in the decades ahead. "New opportunities rarely fit the way an industry has always approached the market, defined it, or organized to serve it," so wrote Drucker in the "Discipline of Innovation." Will IEDC's next generation be defined by world-class leadership in art and management development? By breakthroughs in the development and teaching of sustainability and social entrepreneurship? Or in a space and ways as yet undefined and awaiting its creative leadership?

Quoting American transcendentalist Henry David Thoreau, Danica has created a legacy to guide IEDC forward: "Do not worry if you have built your castles in the air. They are where they should be. Now put the foundations under them."

Legacy

Danica Purg was awarded 2010 Dean of the Year by the Academy of International Business at its meeting in Brazil. In recognizing her, the AIB cited five reasons: (1) The pioneering work she has done founding management education in Slovenia, (2) The important contribution she has made by founding and extending CEEMAN, (3) Recognition of her never ending desire and ability to support others, with the result that she is a role model par excellence for deans, faculty members, and managers throughout the region and beyond, (4) Her innovations in how management education is conceptualized, designed, and delivered, (5) Her contribution to having the world recognize the powerful role that management education plays in the functioning of civil society....

Her legacy, and IEDC's, is also evident in the marks left on MBAs and program participants. To close Part I of this learning history, listen to two reflections from next-generation business leaders on what they will never forget:

> There is no simple formula for change, so the question is how we drive change and lead through change. I believe that change is driven through individual and collective courage, will, decision making power, and drive; and through the ability to direct but also to inspire our surroundings. Empty words? Not to me!
>
> Integrate what you believe into every single area of your life. Take your heart to work, and ask the most and best of everybody else too. Don't let your special character and values, your truth--don't let that get swallowed up by the great chewing complacency. This we've been whispered to during our classes here.

Prof. Joe Pons in the MBA Class

Prof. Leonid Evenko, President of RABE, the opening of IEDC in Bled, 2000

President of the IEDC building committee Mr. Boris Zakrajšek, and the Vice-president Mr. Mirko Kaluža, 2000

Prof. Randy Kudar at IEDC MBA graduation day, 2001

MBA graduation ceremony reception on IEDC terrace, 2005

Gusti always taking care of IEDC participants and guests

Prof. Lynn Isabella with Darden Business School students at IEDC, 2002

Prof. Bill George, President of Medtronic, lecturing at Presidents' Forum, 2002

Mr. Metod Dragonja, president of Lek and president of IEDC Supervisory Board, 2002

Visit of Dr. Vaira Vike Freiberga, President of Latvia, 2002

Prof. J.B. Kassarijan at the graduation of Discover Management Program (DMP), with Prof. Nenad Filipović and Ms. Nataša Mithans, 2003

MBA Graduation 2003, Graduation gowns designed by Mr. Alan Hranitelj

With Mrs. Majda Širca, MP, and Prof. Vojteh Ravnikar, the IEDC architect, 2004

Prof. Pedro Nueno at the conference Bled to Europe, Europe to Bled, 2004

Prof. Aleksandra Kornhauser Frazer receiving Doctor Honoris Causa title, 2007

Dr. Erhard Busek, former vice-chancellor of Austria and president of IEDC Supervisory Board, 2005

REFLECTIONS

→ NETWORKING - THE WAY TO SUCCESS

Danica Purg

Looking back at the 25 year history of our school—which is at the same time a big part of my personal history—I see how networking and my eagerness to network were important for its growth and success.

When I was in secondary school, I was already discovering the value of networking. I became a member of the United Nations Clubs Organization which brings together youth interested in international politics to meet one another, travel, and learn from leaders in business, government, and civic life who shared with us their international experience. When I was 16, I became the president of this organization in Maribor, the second biggest city in Slovenia. I met the American ambassador, functionaries of IAEA (International Atomic Energy Agency), and many other people interested in international relations. I quickly discovered that networking opens up new vistas and can create a fabric of personal contacts that provide resources, information, and often insights, as well as personal support and feedback.

Today, I often talk to students and executives in IEDC programs about the importance of building networks for their personal and organizational development. Networking is a learning process which demands a lot of energy, entrepreneurship, openness for change, passion, courage, and perseverance. You are meeting new people, who may or may not be open to you. Often they are busy, or difficult to engage. You have to know what you want from others and to be ready to offer something, often something more, in return. But, of course, sometimes new connections open up unimagined possibilities.

In networking you have to demonstrate ethical behavior, otherwise people won't trust or respect you and, in order to be successful, you have to constantly use and develop your communication skills. Talking to leaders, I often point out the importance of building a rich and diverse network—reaching out to new fields and new territories—because I see in my professional career and in building up our school how this was important. I would say that personal commitment to hard work and to excellence impressed many people who entered my network, so much so that they were ready to support me and the school "forever."

Early Networks

Networking at an early age not only builds lifelong friendships, it also helps you to define "who you are" and "what you might become" in your career. After completing high school in Maribor, for example, I went to Ljubljana, the capital of Slovenia, mostly because it was a bigger town, providing more chances to meet people and more chances to learn. There I started to build up my network with artists because of having a wish to become a theatre actress (a wish that I had to give up because I didn't get a scholarship). I often went to the Academy of Performing Arts and watched the exercises, made friends with theatre people, and learned how the theatre and dance can stimulate, challenge, and move you. When I later met Arnold, I became more interested in visual arts.

While I am not an artist today, in the professional sense, I have continued to build a network of performing artists and made art and leadership a defining characteristic of management development in our school. A colleague suggested that without me finding my passion for the arts, and having early experiences being with artists and learning from them, it is not as likely that IEDC would be getting "rave reviews" for our innovative arts and leadership programs today.

In Ljubljana, I also had a great network of journalists because I earned my student living by editing international news for the newspaper *Mladina* (the Youth) and contributed also to *Delo* (Labor, the main daily) and other newspapers. This furthered my knowledge and my interest in the "big world" around me. At IEDC today, program participants have daily access to the *Financial Times*, *Wall Street Journal*, and *Inter-*

national Herald Tribune. It is important for them to also develop a "global mind." Of course, many today get their news "on line" and connect to others through Facebook, Twitter, Google Groups, and the like. Fortunately, we have a strong IT and public relations team that keeps us up-to-date on social media.

Working in Belgrade, which was then the capital of Yugoslavia, really opened up my own mind. I entered a network of professors of philosophy, sociology, political science, and international law, giving me a kind of liberal arts education that stimulated my appetite for lifelong learning. I also met many politicians because I worked as a Slovene representative in federal politics. From this time on I still keep some important contacts with politicians from all places of former Yugoslavia. You see them on our Supervisory and International Advisory Boards, in our programs in Bled, as well as Sarajevo, Dubrovnik, and elsewhere, and in conferences throughout Central and Eastern Europe (CEE). I have learned that while building a network is important, maintaining it is even more so.

Building the IEDC Network

I really became a student of networking 25 years ago when the school was launched. I had to find professors, business people, and students, raise funds, work the political angles, and then maintain contact with alums, visiting faculty, and friends, and extend our reach. In the *Harvard Business Review*, Herminia Ibarra and Mark Hunter report that leaders need three types of network to get be successful: operational, personal, and strategic networks. The operational network helps in managing current internal responsibilities and ensures coordination and cooperation among people in the organization. For me, personal networking, which engages people outside of your organization, was always the most important for learning and personal growth. When I started the school, however, I really saw the importance of strategic networks. These plug you into a set of relationships and information sources that broaden your perspective, shape your vision, and empower you internally and externally to achieve personal and organizational goals. Ultimately, key people in your strategic network become important stakeholders in your enterprise.

I also read that the key to strategic networking is leverage—strategic networkers use indirect influence to convince one person in their network to get someone else, who is not in the network, to take action. This enables leaders to marshal information and support to enlist people and institutions to grow their network and extend it to new interests and regions. Five years ago, Nina Bandelj, a Slovene sociologist who worked as the first young researcher at IEDC, and I conducted a study of how private business schools in CEE countries (including IEDC) used networks to build their capabilities, establish their identity and legitimacy, and expand their markets. We also found that many of these schools, like IEDC, also adopted a network form of organization.

Here I want to share some personal stories about creating networks. (See the "map" of all of the stakeholders in my network.) It shows some of the people and institutions that helped in the founding of IEDC, in teaching and learning, and in building and growing the school. Many of these stakeholders of course assumed multiple functions in developing the school.

Enlisting Professors

The most challenging task in the newly established school was to find the best professors. Being a rather small school, we could not afford to employ them full- time. And we didn't have the most attractive value proposition to gain their interest: Who would have come 25 years ago to teach in a small school developing under the umbrella of the Slovene Chamber of Commerce, operating out of hotel in Brdo pri Kranju, with only ten employees and a director, limited financial resources (the first annual budget was around 600,000 German Marks which means today 300,000 Euro), and one classroom for 30 and one for 20 people in the same hotel?

Options in the local market and CEE countries were limited because the educational program would be in English and our aspirations were to open managers' eyes and prepare them to operate in the context of the European and world market. We also wanted to introduce new ways of learning about management and faculties in CEE countries that were very traditional in their teaching methods (mostly lectures).

So I went to different conferences and management schools, visiting first INSEAD and some years later IMD Lausanne, and I learned quickly a key principle of leverage that "first class people bring first class people." The new friends who came were ready to help us further and brought to us their friends and colleagues, and so the network of foreign faculty was growing. We received them warmly, made them feel that they were a part of a very important project, and at the same time we showed them around and put them in touch with business people and a region that they did not know before. For many this became a new enriching experience. (Some of them described our management team as "Amazons" in the early days because we were mostly woman and strong leaders. It was new for them to see women in leadership positions!)

Most of these professors are still with us or were with us for a very long time. I should also mention the contributions of Prof. Aleksandra Kornhauser, former minister of science in Slovenia, and Horst Weitzmann, a German entrepreneur, who enhanced our programs with their practical experience and wisdom. Our MBAs were for several years in a row for a week guests of Mr. Weitzmann and his wife Marlis in Germany. I learned through these great connections that you have to perform well and innovate regularly to keep a network relevant and thriving.

I also believe that, despite electronic communications technology, personal contacts are indispensible. Little touches, like meeting visiting faculty at the airport, greeting them with flowers, taking them to visit the market in Ljubljana, and so on, were a courtesy and made our relationships more personal. Showing our personal attention to visiting faculty is an important way for us to thank faculty for coming to help us. It is not something that they typically see in their own schools and workplaces.

Gaining Political Support

Gaining the support from politicians and other public personalities was very important at the beginning of our school. However, in those socialist times, discussions about starting a "management" school were not so open, and I could not have much of a direct influence on those networks. What proved important was that Marco Bulc, President of the Slovene Chamber, remembered me from Belgrade where he was the Deputy Prime Minister of Yugoslav Federal Government and he gained the impression that I could cope with the challenges of making the school. Relationships with Slovene President Stanovnik and later with President Kučan were rather natural ones because I felt that they were both interested in bringing up better leaders for a better future. They readily gave their support to the school. My most friendly relationship has been with the current president of Slovenia, Dr. Danilo Türk whom I knew already from our youthful activities in the club of the United Nations Organization.

Engaging Business Partners

Throughout these years, relationships with corporate partners have been crucial to the school's development and growth. They provide financial resources, participate in our programs, send employees to us as students, host MBA student projects, underwrite conferences and community service programs, and offer their advice on curriculum and innovations. Many of them have partnered with us on "tailor-made" programs.

In the beginning, most our corporate partners were in Slovenia. This heritage is important because twenty-nine of them became "shareholders" in the school by investing in IEDC when we became independent from the Chamber. Today we partner with many companies throughout Europe and beyond in our corporate programs.
When I talk to students about founding our school and building relationships with businesses, they often ask me about what I say and how I address corporate partners to get their attention and financial support. They are surprised by my answer that there are no special words or expressions required, and that no special prom-

ises or "secret deals" are made. Instead, I invite companies to be partners in an ethical, long-term engagement and in a purposeful and successful project of which they can be proud and can use to develop their people and themselves.

Of course, we have to deliver a successful program. But what matters, too, are good, open, and regular communications and maintenance of the relationship by special attentions, like sending books and articles to partners on topics that you believe would be useful for them to learn more about, writing them a card, visiting their companies, and so on. The best relationships are long-lasting ones. To maintain them we have to understand the businesses and their challenges and we have to be innovative to continue to be of interest to them. This means, like one of our visiting faculty always says, you have to show that you care about them.

Students and Alumni

Our team is always recruiting new students to come to the school. We run special seminars in Slovenia and all over CEE to introduce the school to prospective students and to meet prospective corporate partners. Our website is constantly updated with "news" about what is happening at the school and developments in our programs. And we have marketing and support teams for our courses and custom-made programs. This operational network has to be active and effective for the school to succeed.

Another important network that we built at IEDC throughout 25 years is composed of our alumni—students who studied at our school. The most connected members are the ones who spent the longest time at IEDC, in an MBA or five-week General Management Program, or graduates of the Young Managers Program who are shocked to discover at our school—soon after graduating from their different universities—a much more intense, engaging, and often fun-filled educational experience. They become the school's ambassadors and help to recruit new students via "word of mouth." We also have alumni associations in the region to maintain our relationships with current alumni and to help us to recruit future ones.

Innovative teaching and personal attention are the hallmarks of our school in these programs and also in the Discover Management Programs where undergraduates get their first exposure to management-in-action by creating their own business. Many former IEDC students have become creators of change in their own environments– their organizations and their countries–and it is important to stay in touch with all of them but especially with those that at really "making a difference." It is rewarding for me to go to international conferences and meet alumni who have become members of parliaments, government ministers, presidents of important companies, entrepreneurs, and the like. We are of course very proud of them and especially so when see that they have succeeded ethically.

Growing IEDC and Myself

I must not forget to mention some networks that would qualify as "personal networks" and later became "strategic networks" that helped to grow the school. First, there was the building up of the Central and Eastern European Management Association (CEEMAN) which was established to build relations among deans of management schools in CEE countries and to upgrade the quality of management education in this part of the world.

Here again, as they say, what is most important is your first network partner. So I took building this network very seriously and sought out the best people who knew and could further enlist more of the best people to create the CEEMAN network. We succeeded in bringing together the best deans from the best CEE business schools and later some of IEDC's best professors to launch the CEEMAN International Management Teachers Academy. In this way, CEEMAN developed a critical mass of talented people (network nodes) that attracted more interest and expanded our influence throughout the region and worldwide. In CEEMAN we have today 192 members from 48 countries, two thirds of them come from Central and Eastern Europe and one third are from the rest of the world.

CEEMAN provides intellectual stimulation, teaching resources, and research opportunities to member schools through its teaching academy, research programs, executive development conferences, and publications. There is also an annual gathering of deans and presidents of the business schools where we present the Champion Awards to the top schools, best teachers, outstanding researchers, etc. CEEMAN also provides social support, camaraderie, and a sense of identity for its members. We take care that the meetings (so far we have had 20 conferences in many different countries) are a success; we organize gala dinners with live music and in this way also build very good relationships. We often say: "Come, join our Association, we shall dance together!"

The CEEMAN network and our school, too, which is its hosting headquarters, gets the attention of the international media, publishers, business people, and professors from around the world who come to lecture or participate in programs and share experiences. This keeps the network pulsing. It also reminds me of another rule about networking, which says that if a network is not "working" for your development and interests, it is time to move on. We created CEEMAN back in 1993 because the European Foundation for Management Development wasn't then relevant or responsive to CEE business schools. This is a lesson we keep in mind in globalizing the CEEMAN network today.

Personal Networks

Many of the networks that I entered in the last 25 years and especially in the last 10 involved very important personal relationships that were transformed into strategic networks. I have in mind a great personality, George Soros, and his foundation, the Open Society Institute. The Open Society Institute was launched to help nongovernmental organizations to form or grow to address cultural improvements, especially in areas where local or national governments were not able to support such activities. Joining the Slovenian Board of the Open Society Institute gave me the opportunity to meet many innovators and social entrepreneurs in the region personally in our annual meeting in Budapest. I also got to know Soros who sent me to Russia to visit some institutions that his Foundation financed to check how the money was spent. This was a nice demonstration of the trust that he put in me and I was proud of that.

The Open Society Institute included IEDC in its network of some 20 schools supported by Soros and we were deemed to be a "showroom" for the other schools–showing how to develop faculty, libraries, administration, etc. CEEMAN also got the attention of the Soros Higher Education Support Program (HESP) that helped to fund its teaching academy for CEE faculty and lately also for faculty from Asia and Africa.

Another important personal network which became strategic for our school was the Business Advisory Council (BAC) of the Stability Pact for Southeast Europe, presided over first by German Bodo Hombach, then for longer time by Erhard Busek, the former vice-chancellor of Austria. Busek is a great personality and our region benefited BAC meetings (where I was invited as a representative of Slovenia). I personally learned a great deal from Busek's analysis of the economic and political situation in the region, his vision for its further development, and his ideas for building peace in the Balkans through economic development. Through the BAC, I met the Japanese leaders of Mitsui, a big investor in this part of the world, Coca-Cola president, Mr. Muhtar Kent, who was representing Turkey in the BAC some years ago, and other interesting people. The friendship with Busek developed in such a way that he became four years ago the president of the IEDC Supervisory Board and we continue with him together not only to develop the school but to take actions for progress in the entire region.

One of the latest networks that I built five years ago was when I became a member of the International Advisory Board of the Moscow School of Management Skolkovo where I was invited by well-known businessman Ruben Vardanian on the recommendation of Professor Manfred Kets de Vries from INSEAD. This is a network of top Russian business leaders and politicians. As it is important in every network to first give and then to take resources, I began by helping the management school Skolkovo to develop by sharing my experiences with them, and later had the chance to meet President Medvedev and the elite of Russian business people involved in this school about accreditation and other issues facing business schools around the world.

From this network, I learned about Russia and how business is done there, and I can now comfortably invite Russian faculty, business leaders, and culture figures to IEDC programs or join them in international forums.

Peter Drucker

At the end, I would like to talk about probably the most important meeting for me personally that opened a wide network. It happened in 1995 when I was preparing the 10th anniversary of our school. After asking Henry Mintzberg, John or Nicholas Negroponte, Lester Thurow, and other well-known experts in the field to come to be speakers at our anniversary event, I got an "expensive" answer from each of them. So I decided to contact Peter Drucker and to invite him. After some correspondence I went to visit him and his wife, Doris, in Claremont, California, and we built up a very cordial relationship. I am still in touch with Doris, what a wonderful person!

What I learned from Drucker was how you can be great *and* modest! This connection had symbolic value to IEDC, because people were impressed by our friendship and the attention he gave to our school, and to me personally, when I was invited to speak about him at the 1st Peter Drucker Global Forum in Vienna in 2009. I can also say this helped in forging a strategic network because I am now well connected to Drucker scholars around the world, some of whom have come to our school.

In many respects, IEDC is today a network organization, not only linking our visiting faculty, students, and business partners, as the map of the network shows, but putting our school into a system of networks through CEEMAN and other associations. Great relationships have enabled us to expand through the Japanese Mitsui network to Korea and JETRO (Japan External Trade Organization); through Erhard Busek and

BAC to many companies in Austria; through George Soros and the Open Society network to many talented people and activists around the world; through Skolkovo-Moscow School of Management to Singapore, India, Brazil; and so on. There is, of course, a risk of overload and not being able to properly contribute to or gain from a system of networks. Here I tell fellow managers that the key test is relevance—make sure that your connections are relevant to your personal and organizational development. A give-then-take attitude is required and it is important to remember, as we did in building and growing IEDC, that "only the best is good enough."

I finally must not forget to mention the ideal of "courage." You often have to have the courage to enter a certain network and also to leave it if you see that it doesn't meet your expectations concerning atmosphere, results, and above all ethical standards.

Danica Purg's Network

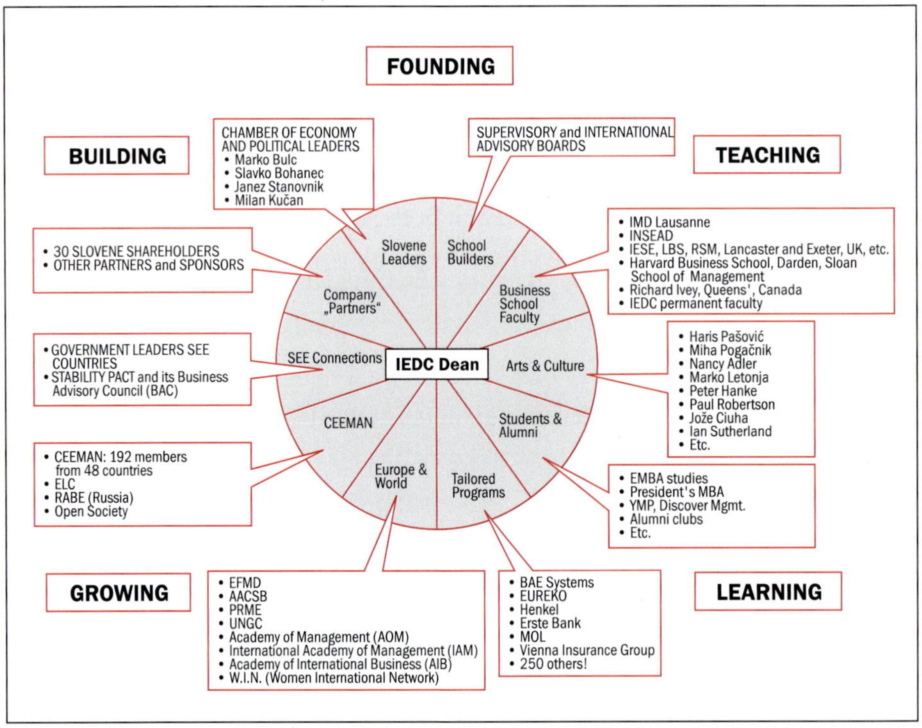

IEDC "BOOKS OF THE YEAR" (1986 - 2010) – A CONTENT ANALYSIS

Arnold Walravens

Since 1988 IEDC has published annually "The Book of the Year," a printed publication of an invited lecture (or set of lectures) by leading academic, business, or political figures on topical subjects. In *The New Realities*, Peter Drucker (who authored the 10th book in this series) writes that management is "what tradition used to call a 'liberal art'–'liberal' because it deals with the fundamentals of knowledge, self-knowledge, wisdom, and leadership; 'art' because it is practice and application." IEDC's Books of the Year reflect this tradition by presenting knowledge and insights from thought leaders who also speak to their practical and relevant applications.

The book is offered as a kind of New Year's present to the participants and alumni of IEDC programs, to professors and staff, and to other relations of the school, including political, business, and cultural leaders in Slovenia and around the world. The intent is to enrich, as Drucker would say it, the IEDC community's *weltanschauung* or world view.

On the occasion of the 25th anniversary of the school, the idea came to analyse the contents of the annual "books of the year" in the belief that this could inform and complement the learning history by highlighting which issues and topics have arisen in the formation of modern management and leadership, particularly in Central and Eastern Europe (CEE), in decades past to the present. From my reading of the 22 volumes–stretching from 1988 to 2010–a conclusion can be made that the books offer a compelling chronology on what was on the minds of leaders and managers as they navigated through transformations in the economies, politics, and societies of the region over those tumultuous years.

A number of themes got special attention in particular years–on, say, competition as the market economy first took shape in the region in 1989 and then on risk management when it collapsed in worldwide recession in 2008. The issues that the books examine also took on new contours as changes in circumstances dictated and as understandings of management practices evolved. Discussion of competition, for example, shifted from a local to regional to pan- European to global context over the years. And while early lectures sought to more sharply define the operations of market capitalism the more recent ones seek to redefine it in light of its political, social, and environmental consequences.

Here are the issues and themes that were addressed by books of the year between 1988 and 2010: change, innovation, competition, customers, values and ethics, trust, risk and risk management, and dealing with crisis.

1. Change (mentioned since 1988)

If there is any one word that continuously comes up in the books (lectures), it is "change." Reading the volumes over the years, it is apparent that everything has been changing all the time and that everybody has had to change. And, change has happened between 1988 and 2010. What is striking is how discussion and reality were transformed over those years. Social, economic, and political relations in 1988 compared to those in 2010 are radically different.

In 1988, for instance, the Triade (USA, Western Europe, and Japan) constituted the economic superpowers in the world. This term disappears in the 1990s and books in the new century describe dramatic changes in the global marketplace (Jean-Philippe Deschamps, 2002) and the accelerated pace of change around the world (Manfred Kets de Vries, 2004). In the past few years, the BRIC countries, particularly China and India, are noted as rising economic powerhouses and an integral part of the business landscape.

What does this mean for practice? In 1988 one can find a carefully formulated statement that socialist systems ought to introduce leadership concepts and methods that were proven successful in capitalist systems (Peter Kraljič, 1988). However, seeing how uncritically the "American model" was propagated by Western experts to collapsing socialist economies, the book of the year of 1992 names it a "stupidity" to transfer ideas and concepts from America and the West to CEE countries (Thomas J. Peters, 1992).

Throughout the 1990s, CEE countries went through a difficult period of restructuring (shock therapy) and had to develop new economic policies and systems of corporate governance. Each country and its companies tried to resolve dilemmas between traditions versus change, between being culturally recognizable and yet different from the past. This issue comes partly as the conclusion in the book of 2001, when the statement was made that "companies in East and Central Europe are normal companies"–although suffering from some deficits in their social and economic system (Milan Kučan, 2001). This book of the year celebrated successes but called out for further improvements in business management and especially in government administration. The point was also made that what is important to success is not the size of a country, but its policies and capacities to adapt to change.

2. Leadership (since 1989)

The words "leading" and "leadership" were highlighted first in the 1989 book of the year. This publication heralded the reformulation of the (Slovene translated) "Centre for Development of Leading Workers" and stated that "new leadership" models and practices (Danica Purg, 1989) would be needed in Slovene companies. In the first years of the new school, the word "management" was a taboo as being understood as a "technocratic" concept. By 1992, however, the book of the year could be addressed to *Developing Managers for Central and Eastern Europe*.

In 1997, leadership came back in attention in the book of the year, not as an organisational concept but as a psychological phenomenon, with a lecture on personal leadership*: Manage Yourself and Then Your Company. Set an Example* (Peter F. Drucker, 1997). The next year's book dealt with the question how a leader can maintain personal value (Pedro Nueno, 1998). The topic of leadership returned regularly in the books of the year afterwards: in a lecture in 2001 as the "innovative imperatives of leadership "(Peter J. Rohleder, 2001) and in 2004 as *The Bright and Dark Sides of Leadership* (where leadership failure factors included an inability to say "no," micromanagement, lack of delegation, and unplanned succession). Again, a personal aspect was given attention to leadership in stressing the importance of "life balance."

Leadership was returned to the grand scale in later books with the existential question "What is in fact leadership?" (Ichak Adizes, 2006) and practitioners were challenged to understand their own style of exercising influence and power.

3. Innovation (since 1989)

Already the second book of the year in 1989 gives attention to one of the big issues of the eighties in CEE countries and the Western world: innovation (Derek F. Abell, 1989). And also characteristic of that period is that innovation is defined as primarily a "technical" issue with its specific processes and methods. In the book of the year 1994, the concept of innovation has technical content, too, dealing with innovation of production (William A. Fischer, 1991).

Eight years later we see how the human factor starts to be seen as a very important element, and particularly the role of leadership being one of the "innovation imperatives." In the publication of 2002 a profile is offered of innovation leadership and of the innovative organisation (William George, 2002). In the publication of 2008, the role of leadership is confirmed in the statement "Innovation is a management issue" (William A. Fischer, 2008).

4. Competition (since 1989)

Almost as if a sound from another world, readers of the book of the year in 1989 heard about "growing competition" (Derek F. Abell, 1989). As the market economy and competition have been important topics in programs and lectures at IEDC, the book of the year 1994 again gave this centre-stage, stressing the urgency to be and stay competitive (William A. Fischer, 1994). Five years later, when the challenges of the global markets were being felt strongly, it was stressed, perhaps as an act of encouragement, that "Slovenia as a small country has also the potential to compete in the global race" (John M. Stopford, 1999). This seemed necessary to oppose growing doubts about the strengths of the Slovene economy, not strange in a period of change and restructuring.

In the book of the year 2001, the accent moved from Slovenia and the Slovene economy as a whole to particular sectors or branches with the lecture offering the conditions and tools "to get a leading position in your own branch" (Peter J. Rohleder, 2001). The basis for competition got a drastic change in the book of the year 1999 that pointed out that companies have to come up with a "new value proposition based on intangible assets, harnessing knowledge that is difficult to copy" (John M. Stopford, 1999). In the book of the year 2004 another new element was brought in by saying that competitive advantage could be created by human dimensions—leadership and corporate culture (Manfred Kets de Vries, 2004).

5. Strategy (since 1990)

Although thinking in "plans" was not a new subject even in the times of the socialist self- management, the concept of a "long-term strategy" was a novel one in the CEE when it was introduced in the 1990 book of year (Arnoldo C. Hax, 1990). On the practical side, this volume also presented a framework for designing strategy. The topic came back in another form in the book of the year 1995 which dealt with the opportunities and pitfalls of "strategic alliances" (George Tauscher, 1995)—increasing in their numbers and scale in the CEE in that period and thereafter.

In 2009, the book of the year also introduced the strategies of "hidden champions"—small and mid-size companies that carve out global market niches—a relevant role model for SMEs in CEE countries (Hermann Simon, 2009).

6. Globalisation (since 1993)

The term and phenomenon "globalisation" were mentioned for the first time in the book of the year 1993 together with the statement that Slovenia was a part of Europe and expressing the wish that it be recognised as a modern European country (*The European Presidents' Challenge, Beyond Restructuring,* 1993). In 2002, the ambitions of Slovenia on this front were made clear in the statement that "companies in East and Central Europe are normal companies." This volume also made an important remark about globalisation and leadership: "a global world needs global leaders" (Milan Kučan, 2002).

In the 2003 book of the year, it was pointed out that global leadership would not be only an "organisational" issue, but also one of finding "new leadership paradigms" (Fons Trompenaars, 2003). This work raised important questions about the importance of recognizing national and corporate culture in the development of global leaders.

7. Values and Ethical Standards (since 1993)

The book of the year 1993 shows that the topic of values was an important issue for public debate at IEDC early on. It came up strongly too in 1996's book of the year that celebrated the 10th anniversary of the school. Listen to this IEDC graduate's testimonial: "Needless to say that this journey of ours towards the accomplishment of the EMBA was a challenging one, demanding in effort and time, very tough in projects and studies. Many of my class colleagues didn't believe at the beginning that attending IEDC's EMBA program could transform us into being even better persons and touch us so deeply, as our Dean foretold us at her first appearance. But it happened. Not only did we gain from educational point of view, but also from personal and interpersonal."

More formal attention was given to the importance of European values and human rights in the book of the year 2002. After a period of anomie in many CEE countries, a plea was formulated for building a "common world of values, a world of high ethical standards" (Milan Kučan, 2002). In the search for common values in Europe it was suggested in the book of the year 2003 that the value of Europe could be "respect for differences" (Fons Trompenaars, 2003).

8. Customers (since 1997)

Everybody dealing with business today will probably ask already: "What about the customer?" After 10 years of being focused on fundamental changes in the economic system, with reorganisations of industries and organisations, and with questions about opportunities in an open economy and globalising world, the book of the year 1997 came with this answer to questions about the strengths and weaknesses of the company: "Ask the customers" (Peter F. Drucker, 1997). Till then answers about performance had been looked for amongst experts, consultants, and statistics. Fourteen years later, this approach was confirmed in the statement: "Everything begins with the customer" (William A. Fischer, 2008). In the book of the year 2009 the role of the customer was formulated as a dynamic phenomenon defining the activities of companies as a response to changing customer needs (Hermann Simon, 2009).

9. Trust (since 2004)

Although the importance of "trust" animated IEDC since the topic of corporate governance was made a formal part of the program (1989), not until the book of the year 2004, following the financial misdeeds of Enron and the dot.com bust, was trust was mentioned "as a characteristic of a successful company" (Manfred Kets de Vries, 2004). This was repeated in the book of the year 2006, describing trust as "a main element of leadership and business success" (Ichak Adizes, 2006).

10. Risk, Crisis, and Redefining Capitalism (since 2006)

It is not surprising that in the past few years' economic and political climate, IEDC's books of the year have been addressed to themes of risk, crisis, and the future of capitalism. The lecture in 2008 presented new frameworks for "risk and risk management" in the context of the global economic crisis (William A. Fischer, 2008); in 2009 the accent was put on the future through "leadership beyond the crisis" (Hermann Simon, 2009); while in 2010 it was considered sensible to stress that the actual crisis was not something completely new and that a lot could be learned from earlier experiences and solutions (Stéphane Garelli, 2010).

Stepping back, these volumes show how, in both management theory and practice, the world has changed in the last 25 years, and particularly so for the world of IEDC—started in the self- management socialist environment in former Yugoslavia and surrounded by countries with state-socialism and now operating in a globalised, market-oriented environment, in a democratic nation, and in a region still undergoing profound change. The 2010 book of the year shows that capitalism, embraced as the economic systems by CEE countries, is being profoundly shaped by new consumer preferences to do business with environmentally and socially responsible companies and by government's greater participation in the economy. Take a look at how the themes have developed in the books of the year 1988 to 2010 in the three exhibits that follow. They show how IEDC has sought to both represent and inform the issues of the day and derive the best implications for practice over its first 25 years and no doubt in its future.

IEDC "Books of the Year"

2010 Stéphane Garelli, Business as Unusual: Competitiveness Outlook for 2011, and Beyond

2009 Hermann Simon, Role Models of Leadership beyond the Crisis

2008 William A. Fischer, New Generation Innovation

2007 Jean-François Manzoni, How to Avoid the Set-Up-to-Fail Syndrome

2006 Ichak Adizes, What Is a Leader? (a video lecture)

2005 Peter Drucker, Manage Yourself and Then Your Company: Set an Example

2004 Manfred Kets de Vries, The Bright and Dark Sides of Leadership

2003 Fons Trompenaars, The Challenge of Leadership--Visions, Values, Cultures

2002 Milan Kučan, Jean-Philippe Deschamps, William George, Leadership for Innovation

2001 Milan Kučan, Peter Kraljič, Peter J. Rohleder, Competitiveness of Companies in Central and Eastern Europe

2000 Paul Strebel, Focusing on Breakthrough Options 1999 John M. Stopford, Harnessing Organizational Knowledge for Strategic Innovation

1998 Pedro Nueno, Maintaining Your Personal Value

1997 Lecture by Peter F. Drucker on the occasion of the 10th IEDC Anniversary: "Manage Yourself and Then Your Company: Set an Example"

1996 10 Years of IEDC

1995 George Taucher, How to Succeed with Strategic Alliances

1994 William A. Fischer, The New Faces of Manufacturing

1993 The European Presidents' Challenge, Beyond Restructuring

1992 Developing Managers for Eastern and Central Europe

1991 Thomas J. Peters, The American Way of Managing--A Model for the Whole World?

1990 Arnoldo C. Hax, Redesigning of Strategic Concepts and Processes

1989 Derek F. Abell, Management in the Organization of the Future

1988 Peter Kraljič, Ways to Industrial Success

The Main Themes in the Books of the Year 1988 – 2010

First mentioned	Theme	Later mentioned
1988	Change	(1992, 2001)
	↓	
1989	Leadership	(1997, 1998, 2001, 2004, 2006)
	Innovation	(1991, 2002, 2008)
	Competition	(1994, 1999, 2001)
	↓	
1990	Strategy	(1995)
	↓	
1993	Globalisation	(1999, 2004)
	Values and ethical standards	(2002, 2003)
	↓	
1997	Customers	(2008, 2009)
	↓	
2004	Trust	(2006)
	↓	
2008	Risk and risk management Crisis	(2009, 2010)
	↓	
2010	Redefining capitalism	

Important issues in the "Books of the year" 1988 – 2010

1988	1989	1990	1991	1992	1993	1994	1995
• change • transferability of leadership concepts and methods	• technical innovation • growing competition	• long term strategy	• stupidity to transfer ideas and concepts of USA, West Europe, Japan, Asia to CEE countries		• European values and human rights • globalisation	• dramatic change • innovative production • urgency to be and stay competitive	• strategic alliances
1996	**1997**	**1998**	**1999**	**2000**	**2001**	**2002**	**2003**
• Book on 10 years of IEDC	• manage yourself and then the company, set an example • ask customers what are the strengths of the company	• maintaining personal value	• Slovenia has potential to compete in global race • new value proposition on intangible assets, harnessing knowledge that is difficult to copy	• getting a leading position in your branch	• increasing speed of changes • innovative imperatives of leadership • companies in CEE are normal companies • global world needs global solutions	• global world and role of EU • size of countries not important, policies are • plea for building common world of values • a world of high ethical standards	• joining international and new paradigms • core values of Europe: respect for differences
2004	**2005**	**2006**	**2007**	**2008**	**2009**	**2010**	
• competitive advantage created by human dimensions: leadership and corporate value • bright and dark sides of leadership • the failure factor of leadership • life balance	• (reprint of the book of 1997)	• what is in fact leadership • "trust" as a main element of leadership and business success	• how to avoid the set-up-to fail-syndrome	• innovation is a management issue • everything begins with the customer • risk and risk management	• response to changing customer needs • the crisis (leadership beyond the crisis)	• the crisis is not something completely new • redefining capitalism	

→ BEING RELEVANT

Nenad Filipović

In late July 2011, I was introduced to the CEO as I was about to present a complex proposal to establish an internal management development academy for one of the largest banks in Central Europe. He opened the conversation with a short question: "You are the Academic Director of IEDC. What does that mean?" I knew of his reputation as a no-nonsense, numbers-driven, energetic leader brought in to completely turn around the bank. Looking at me, he smiled almost like a boy enjoying his mischief. I guess he must have seen a lot of academics in his career.

I told him I am not a very typical academic, as much as IEDC is not representative of a traditional, "hard core" academic institution. I was lucky to start my career as a researcher and teaching assistant with one of the most brilliant professors of computer sciences in this part of the world. I spent three difficult but fulfilling years with him, not liking the man but getting much more from him than I appreciated at that time. When I moved on to become head of the R&D department in a large regional company, he told me that "I was lost for science." I guess he was right, because while achieving a successful track record in R&D, accumulating intense experiences in more than a decade on a fast track general management career, followed by a decision to join a business school where I have spent more than 20 happy years, I never felt much like a scientist. A builder, maybe, or a teacher in the broadest sense of the word: helping others to achieve their worthwhile goals.

Three small events that occurred in the first few weeks of my first job marked me forever as a teacher. The first one was on my first day at the job, when the professor told an anecdote to the three of us that were his new assistants: "When I was younger, I was grading some exams at home. They were lousy and I kept commenting loudly how awful the results were. My five year old son came to me and said: Father, did you consider teaching them first, and only then giving them the exam?"

The second one was when my best friend and I, asked by our professor to prepare a written exam in a core course for final-year students of computer sciences, decided to come up with something new. Instead of exam questions requiring pages of calculations, we asked a few questions that required only some smart thinking and good understanding of underlying principles. The result was disastrous. More than 90 percent of students failed, as opposed to usual 20 - 30 percent fail rate. The professor was not surprised. In his usual, somewhat cynical tone he said: "I hope you have learned your lesson. Students prefer not to use their brains."

The last event happened a few weeks later, when our faculty got a new Dean. My professor frowned at the choice of his colleagues: "This man teaches in the area of computer sciences from papers that are so old that they have changed their color into yellow."

I believe that as a teacher I have the responsibility to help people learn, to stretch them in order to provoke the highest possible level of learning, and to focus them on matters that deserve to be learned. That is what being a good teacher means and that is what is what I try to achieve for IEDC as its academic director. That is why my answer to the banker was: "My job is to make sure that IEDC does relevant things."

Finding a Balance

Obviously, what seems relevant to me need not be relevant for a banker. Since IEDC earns its money and good reputation by providing services to companies and individuals from the business community, our assumption is that we should better align what is relevant for ourselves with what is relevant in the view of the business community. That, however, is not a trivial consideration. If we follow the old maxim and blindly accept the views held by clients, the question "Do they want what they need and do they need what they want?" becomes legitimate. Actually, I have been in many situations when the answer to that question was simply "no," the client was not making the right choice or did not know enough to make an informed decision. At the same time, if we detach from clients and the gap becomes too wide, we risk not truly understanding the client's situation and not being able to convince the client to make a huge and necessary step in a new direction.

That is why we need to balance a fine relationship with our clients, being not too humble and not too arrogant. We have to resolve another paradox at the same time: we must keep a holistic view of the context in which the things are happening and of the issues our clients face while also being able to consider the critical details of the needed content and the process of implementing it. Needless to say, this requires that we are closely connected to the corporate community, both on a personal and institutional level.

This is nothing so new for the world of the business schools. The solutions they adopt, however, are strongly influenced by assumptions they make about the source of relevance.

When looking for the best sources of relevance, traditional business schools put academic research in the forefront. They assume that the research insights are main drivers of new knowledge, and that this new knowledge is the core value needed and appreciated by their clients from the corporate world. I think both assumptions are grossly wrong; and recent developments—from ethical lapses to inability to predict economic crises or to cope with the impact—are manifestations of the questionable relevance of mainstream academic research.

What is behind this strong statement? My concerns have to do with the fragmentation of research, most of which deals with minuscule bits of knowledge, of little relevance for the vast majority of practicing managers ("yellow papers" syndrome), as well as with the attitude that the clients should be grateful for the opportunity to be exposed to this knowledge, regardless of the way it has been conveyed ("teach them before examining" syndrome). Since clients kept their own share of blame for not putting more pressure on academia ("use your brains" syndrome), the circle becomes quite vicious.

While acknowledging the need for well-focused and timely research as one of the necessary ingredients, IEDC took a broader view on the key sources of relevance. Over the last 25 years we have learned to look for knowledge in three main areas, one of which is in the domain of individual faculty members, while the other two are on the institutional level. On the individual level, we expect that all of our faculty members actively engage as advisors to senior executives. In doing that they not only stay in touch with the most pressing issues within their field of interest, but they have to prove the quality of their advice constantly in the open market.

On the institutional level, IEDC has developed two specific lines of activities which serve as powerful links with "real life," while at the same time adding to the quality of learning and management development, as well as creating immediate tangible benefits for our corporate clients. One of them concerns "project-based learning" and the other involves tailor-made programs that we develop for specific needs of individual corporate partners.

Project-Based Learning

We included project-based learning in our educational programs almost at the very beginning of IEDC, starting with the launch of General Management Program (GMP) in 1987. The basic idea of GMP project work hasn't changed since then: every individual participant has to select an issue which is a major managerial priority, analyze the situation, and propose a solution to it. The work is done under the mentorship of one of the GMP faculty, often paired with an internal mentor from the participant's company, and the participants are stimulated to use the fresh learning from the GMP when addressing the issue. At the end they have to make a short presentation to classmates and faculty, as well as a more thorough one within their companies. With more than 1100 GMP projects prepared over the course of 24 years, it is interesting to see how they have changed over time. Of course, the sample of project topics is biased by the makeup of GMP participants, which has changed in an interesting way. In early years, for instance, GMP participants were more or less general managers, typically from small firms, and faced basic business challenges having to do with finance, marketing, and organization. Now we see many more participants coming from positions within technical areas (e.g., R&D, manufacturing, or supply-chain management). Their projects focus on IT, interdepartmental co-operation, and change management. We also see a lot more people from "client interface" areas, with titles that even did not exist in the management dictionary in Central and Eastern Europe (CEE) some 15 years ago (e.g. product, demand, or communications managers).

The topics have become more sophisticated than in the past, in terms of both their complexity and depth. Since the starting level of participants' competences seems to be much higher than in the early days of the program, we find that the company mentors have a more challenging job nowadays: the participants are often more technically and even managerially sophisticated than their bosses! This is especially true for participants coming from multinational or leading regional companies. The drawback, however, is that the "busyness" of these participants prevents some from investing the extra effort needed to achieve results beyond routine expectations and from reflecting more about their leadership in action.

Since GMP projects are prepared by individual participants, they are indicative of challenges these managers face at their jobs, but only indirectly reflect broader issues their companies have to cope with. To better understand these issues, we use another project-based learning vehicle, team learning, in our Executive MBA (EMBA) and Presidents' MBA (PMBA) programs. More than 250 team projects have been undertaken since 1991, when we introduced the first EMBA program. In EMBA projects, a team of 5 to 7 participants work together with a client organization to dig into problems, formulate possible solutions, and engage relevant interests in evaluating them and taking action. PMBA projects are prepared by individual participants but they are supported by their internal, company teams. In terms of the complexity of topics and their strategic importance for the client companies, both types of projects are equivalent.

These projects require significant investment of time: typically more than 300 hours per member of project team, as well as around 50 hours per mentor. The projects open several dimensions of learning for the participants: using their managerial competences in a reasonably safe learning environment, practicing various skills (from analytical and decision making to persuasion and team skills), looking at complex issues from a general management perspective, as well as getting direct feedback about their advisory and leadership performance from their peers, mentors, and client organizations.

IEDC also receives number of benefits: these projects not only allow us to better evaluate the true leadership potential of the participants (quality of project work has been one of the best predictors of their future career patterns), they also engage us in profound conversations with client organizations around issues of strategic importance for them. Clients seem to find that the benefits from these conversations more than outweigh the investments since we often receive requests for new projects from "old" clients.

Although the positive aspects of using projects for individual and institutional learning seem to be compelling, achieving them is far from easy. The fact that IEDC is a boutique school helps because we need only a manageable number of projects for program participants (these days around 15 to 20 projects per year). On the other hand, our small permanent faculty size comes as a handicap. The burden of mentoring cannot be equally spread to all of our faculty, since mentors must have significant time available (thus visiting faculty are not the best choice) and they have to be "da Vincian" types—experienced, all-around players who can comfortably deal with a wide variety of dimensions every project brings along and who can credibly act as counterparts to CEOs of client companies. Of course, faculty mentors can use "semi-standard approaches" developed by IEDC, and they can draw on other faculty members for specialist opinion, as well as on executive coaches for dealing with problematic team dynamics, but they must be ready to steer the projects autonomously and to personally engage on an immediate basis in case of any emergency.

At the same time, these faculty members also learn a lot about management, leadership, and business from their "hands-on" involvement with teams and projects. They also extract institutional learning from the projects and convey it to other colleagues within IEDC, creating part of the needed relevance for our school. In so doing, they also act as the "IEDC face" toward corporate clients, ensuring that they see IEDC as a relevant partner in their efforts. To be successful as project mentors, faculty need to be skillful at managing stakeholders' expectations and creating positive energy around a project and project team. They also need conflict resolution and crisis management skills, since practically all projects include periods of high stress and pose demanding challenges.

Like with GMP projects, the MBA projects are also changing over time. Again, part of the changes may be attributed to higher competence levels of everyone involved, but the other part comes from the changing strategic focus of our corporate clients. In the early 1990s, for instance, most of the projects were dealing with functional improvements (e.g. introducing appropriate cost management, marketing strategies or HR systems), while some others were in the context of survival struggles (e.g. restructuring, cost containment or boosting income from a new product). The topics of the late '90s to a large degree focused on two issues: various aspects of going-to-market, as well as the overall strategic positioning of the company. The next period, from the early 2000s up to the crisis in 2008, there was even more pronounced focus on growth strategies, as well as "soft" topics (e.g. organizational culture, talent management, or organizational learning). The last period was characterized by less emphasis on these softer subjects and more focus on "niche" thinking (e.g. examining of strategic potential of certain product lines) and learning from successful competition.

Although IEDC has gained a high reputation for its MBA projects, improvements are still on the agenda. The level of reflection that should accompany the work on the projects and increase the learning impact is still not sufficient, neither for individual participants nor for IEDC as an institution. Moving "busy managers" (or faculty) into reflection mode is not easy, thus reflective activities must be well structured and facilitated, or they do not reach the desired effectiveness. Also, the dominant mentality of the managers participating in the projects, as well as those being on the receiving end, is geared towards problem solving and fast attainment of tangible results, while we would like to put more emphasis on opening up and using the projects for individual and organizational development, rather than (just) resolving a concrete issue.

Tailor-Made Programs

We also use project based learning in tailor-made programs designed for the specific needs of individual corporate partners. These projects are similar to the ones used in the MBA setting, but engage higher levels of motivation from everyone involved, put the participants under even more time pressure (typically the companies want to achieve the same quality of results with less time allocated for the projects), and put even more focus on achieving tangible and measurable objectives. Not all tailor- made programs include project work because some companies believe that their managers are so busy with projects in their everyday lives that the benefit of adding one more even for learning does not justify the extra burden. While I in principle think differently, I am ready to accept such a position since it usually reflects lack of commitment for this kind of learning at the top of client organization, which in itself would be a critical obstacle to successful implementation.

In my experience, it is exactly the degree of commitment at the top which distinguishes our most successful tailor-made programs from “solid,” but not high- impact ones. We learn most about the real life in client companies and are able to help them best when the top team (or at least the CEO her/himself) believes that an organizational intervention through a tailor-made program is worth the effort, as well as when the CEO is also ready to listen at least to some degree to our thinking about what would work best for the company in a given situation.

Understanding the situation at hand and the client's professed needs are the essential first steps of our engagement, often requiring quite some homework and numerous conversations with the client. It is interesting that only rarely have I heard from clients a clear articulation of their management development needs in the early stage of our relationship (although many strongly believe that "goals are clear"—and they are to the extent that clients come with a readymade design of what they want to purchase). We therefore prefer to talk to managers at different levels of the client organization and avoid making HR professionals the sole interpreters of the desires from the top. We also fight for the opportunity to engage in a candid conversation with the CEO before any final conclusion about program design is made.

Two classes of our interventions usually come up as the essential ingredient of the tailor-made program: developmental and catalytic. The mix between the two can significantly vary from case to case. When we started working with one of the largest FMCG companies in Europe, for example, it became clear to us that the situation asked primarily for the developmental intervention. While their CEE organization (headquartered in Vienna) could send some of the regional managers to the company's Global Academy, the numbers were far from sufficient and the specific regional issues would not be in the program focus. We discussed the needed competences of the target managerial population, the needed number of people to go through the program in order to create impact on the regional level, and the desired teaching style and many other dimensions of the program design. Company representatives "saw in action" all of the proposed faculty members before agreeing to the final roster.

We also jointly developed the material for internal communications, decided on the program name, evaluation methodology, and other issues important for proper implementation. The firm's HR staff attended the first three program runs and we jointly fine-tuned the program. We have since kept meeting annually and reviewing all the critical issues. This autumn the 17th group of 25 managers will join the program, with almost a full year backlog of applicants. While the company was initially looking for a set of "tools" to be acquired by the participants (the initial name of the program was "Strategic Tools"), thus leading to improved managerial knowledge, they admit now that the main organizational impact comes from the broader set of leadership competences, new ways of looking at things, and more positive attitudes acquired by the participants through the program.

While the program has become wildly successful and joining it has almost become the matter of prestige, we are aware that circumstances have changed for our client. From an era of "sky is the limit" growth opportunities in CEE countries, the client is now facing a much more diverse situation in the region, part of it becoming as mature as some West European markets, another part in deep recession, and yet another part still offering potential growth opportunities. The situation is different across different business lines, too, so we see the need to engage not only on the developmental side, but also helping with catalytic interventions, especially when the client organization faces very specific challenges. That is the only way we can stay relevant for clients, although it may require for them some risky and painful adjustments.

Catalytic interventions are exactly what two of our major clients requested, understanding that they each had problems with corporate identity as side effects of numerous M&A activities. While seemingly simpler, these kinds of programs require not only good initial diagnostics of the situation in a client organization, they also demand educational materials—case studies, exercises, discussion topics—appropriate to the issues at hand and extremely skillful facilitation by faculty and program coaches. We have to challenge often hard-nosed and cynical company executives to come up with real issues, help them to deal with them openly and positively, and then provoke them to leave the program with a renewed emotional contract. This can't be achieved through routine educational curriculum or consulting workshops, but asks for creative approaches that involve, in the workings of IEDC, high-energy cases, facilitated dialogues, times for personal reflection, and exposure to new ways of learning, as outlined by my colleagues on the faculty in their chapters.

The success of our tailor-made programs and our resulting relevance in the eyes of corporate clients starts by us using well the opportunity to come close to them with our hearts, eyes, and ears open (rather than with our mouths talking). After that, success follows the old PIE (Performance, Image, Exposure) paradigm: 1) we perform well on a daily basis, often leading participants to say that our program was one of the most memorable experiences in their life; 2) we carefully build our reputation with client organizations and make our programs desired by their managers, which creates a good image and motivates managers to want learn more; and 3) we strive to bring the best in management thinking and pedagogy to our programs, while honestly serving the changing needs of different stakeholders. All of this builds a long-lasting relationship where IEDC and clients become "us," rather than "we and they."

→ ON FALLING IN LOVE

Nadya Zhexembayeva

There is no question that many found my 2007 decision to move to Slovenia surprising. After 10 remarkable years in the United States—filled with great projects, communities, and organizations—an idea of moving to a boutique business school in a barely-know country seemed, to put it lightly, unexpected. Colleagues, friends, family, and perfect strangers all demanded a clear answer to an understandable question. Why?

The truth is: I fell in love. Nothing less, nothing more. I fell in love.

I remember exactly how it happened. My husband and I came to visit IEDC on Lake Bled for a short weekend. After three flights and a late-night arrival, we woke up to a remarkable view of a 1000-year-old castle bathing in a soft sunrise. A guest lecture was my first job of the day. As a way of getting to know the IEDC audience, I chose to speak about Appreciative Inquiry—a unique approach to strategic management and organizational development that goes against most of the assumptions about management and change. The room was filled with senior executives—focused, alert, and surprisingly present. As our conversation quickly gained depth, I found myself moved by their remarkable hunger and honesty. Here was a not-so-easy crowd, yet there was nothing artificial about our time together. I loved it.

As we parted happy and intrigued with each other, the school's president, Danica Purg, and her husband, Arnold Walravens, whisked us away for a trip exploring the country. We drove through the endless hills and quiet valleys, listening to the history of the land and the history of the school. An incredible discovery was unfolding. Here was a story of collapse and emergence, breaking and building, disconnecting and interconnecting. Here was a school, born amidst a crush of socialism, daring to mold its reality, its region, its world. I was inspired.

From the mountains to the sea and back to the mountains, our trip rounded up with another lecture—on the turbulent subject of sustainability. As we discussed the new environmental and social challenges reshaping—if not revolutionizing—the business reality of today and tomorrow, the questions cut through the simplified definitions of corporate social responsibilities, shooting straight to the essence, nature, and purpose of business. A small dinner with Danica followed, filled with jokes, invitations, and profound insights. When the taxi took us back to the hotel, she stayed on the parking lot, waving kisses and goodbyes. Here was a person putting her life on the line for something so much bigger than her own self. I was crying.

And so, I fell in love. I still am.

Appreciative Inquiry

Remarkably, those very first topics I brought to IEDC in 2007 continue to echo throughout the school and my own work here. Perhaps, right this moment, as you are reading these words, in a sun-lit classroom of IEDC a group of senior managers is hard at work. At a first glance, the intense discussions and strong arguments might appear as a typical problem-solving exercise: take a problem, understand the factors of failure, and propose a decision. But if you listen closely, you might find yourself amidst a very different conversation.

What is unfolding in front of you is a process of Appreciative Inquiry (AI)—a change management methodology celebrated as one of the most important innovations in strategy and organizational development of the past decade. Just like the traditional change management process, Appreciative Inquiry addresses a problematic area of company performance—whether it is productivity, customer satisfaction, cost efficiency, or any other domain. But unlike the traditional problem solving, AI looks for answers in less than obvious places. Instead of analyzing past failures in an attempt to improve performance, through the process of Appreciative Inquiry managers systematically search for and analyze past successes—and companies from Wal-Mart to Ernst & Young are buying in.

So, what does this shift look like, exactly?

When a major airline experiences excessive baggage loss, it is tempting to focus on failure trying to understand what the company is doing wrong. Appreciative Inquiry shifts the focus of analysis from the extraordinary baggage loss towards extraordinary arrival experiences—systematically finding and analyzing situations when a passenger had an exemplary arrival even when all circumstances, from bad weather to air traffic, worked against the company.

For a car service company striving for 100 percent customer satisfaction, it is normal to look into each lost or dissatisfied customer, searching for reasons for failure. Appreciative Inquiry challenges the company to deeply understand reasons behind each loyal and satisfied client, assuring that there is a compelling reason for every customer to stay with the company in the future.

For a specialty coffee company going through rapid growth, costs are the name of the game. Instead of focusing on inefficiencies, Appreciative Inquiry invites the company to find best but underutilized methods throughout all major practices, and makes such cost-saving practices become a norm, rather than exception.

Whether it is manufacturing or services, small or large, for all organizations the discoveries and results of Appreciative Inquiry differ drastically from traditional strategic change efforts. When we focus on what we are doing wrong, we paradoxically become experts in mistakes: they let us know to the last little detail of how to do what is wrong, but tell us little about how to do what is right. Appreciative Inquiry allows us discover the right course of action in a systematic and comprehensive way, which is only possible where we shift the focus, and re-frame the question of our inquiry. When we address the issue at hand by ignoring the cases of past failures, and focusing instead on examples where similar issues were resolved successfully, not only do we find surprising answers, but also energize employees, foster creativity, and avoid "blame games" among a team, thus assuring successful turnaround in a change process.

And what about results? For an approach traditionally perceived as "soft," Appreciative Inquiry has had a remarkable track record. Just a short sample of tangible financial results suggest the strong case for AI: for Hunter Douglas's Window Fashions Division, using Appreciative Inquiry in a business process improvement initiative generated savings of $3.5 million in the first year; Green Mountain Coffee Roasters successfully achieved its "25c Challenge," which allowed for reduction of operating costs by 25 cents per pound of coffee, approximately a 7 percent reduction in gross costs. Managers of Santa Ana Star Casino believe that Appreciative Inquiry was instrumental in driving revenues and achieving profit turnaround of $10 million USD in 2003. Ernst & Young added Appreciative Inquiry to its toolbox, while Wal-Mart has used it in its change management efforts for sustainability. GTE, British Airways and NOKIA continue the list, all suggesting that the time might come to start looking for our answers in less than usual places.

With IEDC's relentless backing, I have been doing just that for four years now. Appreciative Inquiry and strength-based change have become an integral part of leadership and organizational behavior courses at Bled, while each year we bring European change makers and organizational strategists for seminars and conversations on the subject. I am happy to say that my American mentors—David Cooperrider and Ron Fry—continue to lend a hand in this effort and travel faithfully to the little Alpine lake. We keep the coffee warm for both of them.

Embedded Sustainability

Another colleague and dear friend—Chris Laszlo—has been my partner-in-crime with the second theme embraced by IEDC. The school has made a firm decision to embed sustainability—strong environmental and social performance—into all aspects of its work, including teaching, research, and school operations. Complex and interdisciplinary in nature, sustainability challenges have to be addressed across functions and disciplines. But even more so, if the experience of IEDC is of any indication, a whole system approach is required if our efforts are to have any impact.

For us at IEDC, focusing on our students alone did not bring desired outcomes; in contrast, managers felt rather frustrated as they returned from their studies and attempted to apply the new knowledge to the old social and environmental challenges. As result, we decided to approach our sustainability efforts via three interdependent areas of activity:

- *Manager*: supporting development of sustainability attitudes, knowledge, and skills at the individual level;
- *Company*: creating a supportive organizational environment for individual managers ready to lead sustainability change;
- *Society at Large*: investing in development of mutual understanding, common vision, and good will for business-led sustainability efforts within the general society.

And this tall-order holistic approach dared me to take sustainability thinking seriously—by doing some serious thinking about it. *Embedded Sustainability: The Next Big Competitive Advantage*, co-authored with Chris Laszlo and published by Stanford University Press and Greenleaf Publishing, offered our own attempt to make sense of a rapidly changing world.

In recent years, three big sustainability trends—declining resources, radical transparency, and increasing expectations—have redefined the way we do business. We are running out of resources (and the erratic prices for everything from oil to tomatoes are a testament to that decline); we are facing new demands from customers, investors, and governments alike; and we have to figure it all out while being under the microscope of NGOs, media, and society at large. With these new pressures on our hands, what is business to do?

You might have noticed that sushi restaurants now regularly post *toro*, the fatty cut from the belly of the prized Bluefin tuna, at "Market Price." Traveling in airports around the world, you will also find it marked "Unavailable" on the menu. In all but the Antarctic waters the Bluefin has been so heavily overfished that stocks are now at less than 10 percent of what they once were. It has become so rare that a single, healthy-sized tuna recently fetched $396,000 USD in Tokyo's largest fish market.

Bluefin tuna is just one visible example of the decline of natural resources, from clean water and top soil to food crops, fossil fuels, and biodiversity. During the 2007-2009 downturn, the World Wildlife Fund, a leading environmental conservation organization, warned that "the possibility of financial recession pales in comparison to the looming ecological credit crunch." The signs of a crisis in natural resources are starkly evident: the Commodity Price Index, a measure of price movements for 22 commodities, has more than tripled since 2002 and in 2010 alone rose 27 percent with commodities such as cotton rising almost 100 percent. Combined with higher- than-average price volatility, these upward price trends and growing scarcities pose a serious challenge for the security of supply chains.

To declining natural resources, we add two more trends: radical transparency and rising expectations. Fueled by unprecedented activism in the civil sector and enabled by rapid developments in information technology, transparency has become the dynamic, immediate, and substantive force of modern corporate life. It enables any interested person to peer into product and service lifecycles and find those impacts on society and nature that used to be hidden from public scrutiny. The third trend– rising expectations–invites companies to re-think the very essence of market demand. Investors, employees, and, most importantly, consumers increasingly expect sound social and environmental performance. New parameters are becoming standard, such as quiet, healthy, socially equitable, or environmentally-friendly for every product and service in the economy. We don't want just any household cleaning product; we want it non-toxic and biodegradable. We drink fair trade coffee and bring reusable shopping bags to the supermarket. And we no longer accept to pay more for these attributes.

For some, these three trends present an immense threat to be countered at every turn. For others, it's the opportunity of a lifetime. The question is only: do we choose to ride this new wave on our own terms, or become its victims as the tsunami reaches our shores?

In response to these mounting pressures, the majority of managers continue with the familiar approaches to sustainability in business, treating new social and environmental demands as annoying obligations to be addressed by a marginalized corporate social responsibility program. Then there are some that now recognize social and environmental performance as a business opportunity, but they mostly continue to "bolt it on" to existing strategy and operations. Remember all those solar panels and two-sided copying promoted at the office headquarters of a dirty manufacturing business? Way too often we just keep bolting it on!

Only a handful are choosing to embed sustainability into the very DNA of what they do, incorporating environmental, health, and social value into core business activities with no trade-offs in price or quality—with no green or social premium. The Nissan Leaf, a 100 percent electric car named World Car of the Year 2011, offers features at a price found for most gasoline powered cars. Combined with the emerging infrastructure to recharge electric cars, Nissan's multi-billion euro investment is driven by the quest for industry leadership, not selling eco-cars to environmentalists.

Unlike the bolt-on approaches, embedded sustainability requires a fundamental shift across every dimension of the business system:

Bolt-On vs. Embedded Sustainability: Key Dimensions

	Bolt-On Sustainability	Embedded Sustainability
goal	Pursue shareholder value	Pursue sustainable value
scope	Add symbolic wins at the margins	Transform core business activities
customer	Offer 'green' and 'socially responsible' products at premium prices or with diminished quality	Offer 'smarter' solutions with no trade-off in quality and no social or green premium
value chain	Manage company's own activities	Manage across the product or service life cycle value chain
organization	Create a 'scapegoat' department of sustainability	Make sustainability everyone's job

Leading companies such as Unilever, General Electric, Clorox, HSBC, and many others are learning to leverage global challenges, such as climate stability, for enduring profit and growth. The key to making it work is innovation—in product designs, processes and business models—enabling these companies to create even more value for their customers and investors than they otherwise would.

Let me put it in a different way. We know how to meet the demands of shareholder value—years of managerial excellence testify to this achievement. We also know how to create stakeholder value: traditional approaches such as CSR and philanthropy that predictably lead to added costs. Favoring one or the other produces a growing number of bolt-on sustainability efforts resulting in fragmentary efforts and symbolic wins at the fringes of the company.

What we are still discovering is how to meet both shareholder and stakeholder requirements in the core business—without mediocrity and without compromise— creating value for the company that cannot be disentangled from the value it creates for society and the natural environment. When that is done, your company becomes untouchable—as such competitive advantage is nearly impossible to imitate. For myself, my colleagues, and, luckily, at IEDC, embedded sustainability offers you a path towards this advantage, the one that will only grow as today's global challenges continue to deepen.

Design, Inquiry, Appreciation, Wholeness

Now, how do you prepare experienced managers for the challenges of embedded sustainability? While traditional business skills remain vital when embedding sustainability into the DNA of your company, they must be complemented by new competencies. We have found the following four to be essential yet rarely valued in today's corporate world: Design. Inquiry. Appreciation. Wholeness.

Design is first and foremost an attitude or mode of thinking. At its core is an assumption strikingly different from the one that underlies the typical business decision. If decision making is all about making a hard choice between easy-to- identify alternatives, design attitude assumes an easy choice between difficult-to- create alternatives. Tim Brown, CEO and President of IDEO, ranked among the 10 most innovative companies in the world, illustrates this point in the following way: "a management philosophy based only on selecting from existing strategies is likely to be overwhelmed by new developments at home and abroad. What we need are new choices—new products that balance the needs of individuals and of society as a whole; new ideas that tackle the global challenges of health, poverty, and education; new strategies that result in differences that matter and a sense of purpose that engages everyone affected by them. What we need is an approach to innovation that is powerful, effective, and broadly accessible. Design thinking...offers just such an approach."

The next two competencies—*Inquiry and Appreciation*—build respectively on what is possible and on the existing strengths present in every business system. That is why the love for Appreciative Inquiry, which I already shared with you earlier, is a perfect complement to our sustainability work. Efforts to discover and elaborate the positive core—the past, present, and future capacities of the whole system—lead to innovations that integrate societal stakeholder issues that are often excluded from consideration in conventional approaches to decision making.

Wholeness is the final skill needed to master the complex challenge of embedding sustainability across entire business systems. It requires an ability not only to see the big picture, but also to understand the linkages within the system. Donella Meadows, the systems scientist, quotes an ancient Sufi teaching that captures this focus: "You think because you understand one you must understand two, because one and one makes two. But you must also understand 'and'." Learning systems tools such as feedback loops, lifecycle analyses, and stakeholder value maps can help managers develop solutions that are less fragmentary and contradictory than bolt-on sustainability measures developed in isolation. Embedded sustainability continues to make rounds through the walls of IEDC and the companies of its many graduates.

And so you have it, the story of one love. As I finish these reflections on a warm August night, the walls of the school are quiet and full of promise. In only few short weeks, every inch of the space will be filled with ideas, footsteps, and conversations. Appreciative Inquiry, embedded sustainability, and many other efforts will weave together into a beautiful pattern, a fabric of this unique place. Make sure to stop by.

HOW I BECAME INSPIRED BY IEDC, HIDDEN CHAMPIONS, AND JAMES MARCH

Melita Rant

Major transitions in my life were always initiated by events and people that inspired me most and at the right moment. Exactly when facing my biggest doubts, these inspirations came at the right moment.

One of the people that inspired me was James March. In 2006, I attended an Organization Science conference celebrating his ideas in organizational decision making. At the time, I had just finished my Ph.D. at the Faculty of Economics in Ljubljana, studying adaptations of medium and large Slovenian companies to the new competitive landscape that resulted from the more open, market driven economy and Slovenian admittance of the EU. I had become tired of reading "boring" academic articles and of writing academic papers that even I did not care to read once published. I also had serious doubts whether I wanted to become an academic. What I had liked most about my Ph.D. studies were the ideas of March, so it was natural for me to apply for the conference dedicated to him. Once I heard his lecture about Don Quixote—about the passion and discipline Quixote exerted to follow his (foolish?) dreams and yet also be more truthful to himself than any of the other reasonable men he encountered in his journeys—I began to cry. I thereafter read works on decision making and human nature by March, Karl Weick, Henry Mintzberg, and other management scholars.

Though I read these academic works with curiosity, I still carried doubts about my academic career. I did not see any real impact to my teaching organizational theories to graduate students in economics. Then, in 2008, I participated in CEEMAN's International Teachers Academy—loving the classes; crying again at the closure. I experienced my second "AHA" inspiration: understanding that being a teacher of management can be interesting, if done properly, for both teacher and students! Luckily, an opportunity to join the IEDC came across; I grasped it and started developing myself in more participant-centered teaching. Though I was trying out teaching in different fields, from Leadership to Accounting, none really fitted my shoes, which was felt in the classroom.

Then, in October 2009, when recession started to loom more severely over CEE countries, Hermann Simon, an internationally recognized management scholar, was invited to speak at IEDC's Annual Presidents Forum about lessons from the most "recession proof" companies, which he named hidden champions. Hidden champions are companies focused on narrow niches that: 1) hold number one, two or three in the global market, or number one on their home continent, determined by market share; 2) earn revenues below $4 billion USD, and 3) have low levels of public awareness. I came to Danica Purg with the idea to explore further this group of "recession proof" companies in Slovenia and other CEE countries, and she proposed that we enlist scholars throughout CEEMAN.

Hidden champion: A real phenomenon or a management fad?

Simon came across the idea of hidden champions in early 1990s when he was researching the drivers behind export leadership of Germany economy and the role small and medium size companies (SME) played in this phenomenon. The main finding was that the largest SMEs developed a set of distinctive, highly coherent business practices which were consistent across three pillars of strategic scope: product focus, value chain depth, and regional expansion.

In brief, hidden champions developed a narrow, technically advanced product group tailored for a specific customer group. They integrated backward in their industry value chain to cover all critical phases of product development. To expand internationally, they wanted to preserve their closeness to customers, so instead of using external distributors they grew though own sales subsidiaries. Most importantly, Simon attributed the most important driver of hidden champions' success to company leaders, in most cases entrepreneurial founders who grew the company from scratch.

There were, however, many open questions facing the CEEMAN research team that began its work in summer 2010: could we find hidden champions in CEE countries, understand how they grow with limited resources for international expansion, and identify institutional pillars to support hidden champion type companies to boost the growth of economies?

Hidden champions from CEE: Searching a map full of white spots

Being the main project coordinator, my task was to form a team of 50 researchers from all CEE countries (plus Turkey, Kazakhstan, and Greece, making 21 countries in all), plus define research goals, set up the research methodology with activities and deadlines, and above all coordinate project implementation. Communicating, informing, educating, helping, listening, adjusting to surprises, learning, and pushing, pushing drove the project forward.

Three main obstacles blocked the efficiency of our company search. First, the most obvious and also expected one was that these kinds of companies like to stay hidden. Second, some countries did not have established public reporting practices; so in searching for champions the terrain became covered with fog. And third, even when we managed to crawl through the fog, we did not always find Simon-like champions. The institutional context in CEE countries differs in some key respects– less efficient financial markets, weaker property rights, more ambiguous governance structures, etc.–from the one in Germany and other nations where hidden champions have been studied. So we had to find our own type of hidden champions.

Who are hidden champions from the CEE region?

The CEE researchers identified more than 130 hidden champions (mostly SMEs), which all carried healthy seeds of international competitiveness out of which beautiful trees can grow. Our sample has more diversity than Simon's hidden champions: CEE hidden champions are more variable in size (from 1 to 300M €, with average of 50M €), range from agriculture and metallurgy to information and communication technologies, and most hold niche leadership on a regional level (CIS, Baltic, Western Balkan), yet all are growing in revenues through internationalization. Many integrated forward into more value adding areas of their industry value chain. There was also a group of companies that created new products and technologies that resulted in completely novel market niches.

What is the dominant business logic of hidden champions?

To answer this question, I searched for elements of leaders' reasoning and action across success stories of hidden champions companies. The exhibit below compares the dominant business logic of a typical leader-hidden champion with that of a typical executive manager.

Hidden Champions versus Traditional Executives

Leader - Hidden Champion	Traditional Executive Manager
See opportunities	See constraints
Surprise is good	Surprise is bad
Use resources you have	Constrained by resources you lack
Commitment to the world of possibilities	Commitment to current reality
Acts based on intelligent altruism	Acts based on calculative opportunism
Deliberate ignorance of knowledge	Purposeful pursuit of knowledge
Minimizing the affordable loss	Maximizing the expected return

See opportunities where others see obstacles

The first element in the dominant logic of hidden champions, "turning constraints into opportunities," is exemplified by Sandi Češko, an entrepreneurial founder of Studio Moderna, which is nowadays the biggest electronic retailer in CEE and has outperformed competition from North America and Western Europe in the CEE region.

In early 1990s, when direct TV spread to the CEE region, Sandi Češko and his friend Branimir Brkljač established a business venture and bought the property rights for Kosmodisk, a novel device for treating low back pain. When Branimir proposed to try selling Kosmodisk on a direct TV, Sandi's initial response was negative. "TV shopping--no way. Who trusts the products? No one buys products on TV." Then a revelation: Low-trust business is not attractive to competition either. "Wow, it sounds like a perfect barrier to entry! And if we manage to create a brand which customer trust...'" Eventually Sandi's products won customers' trust and Studio Modena grew into a 250m € venture!

Surprise can be good

A second dominant behavior of hidden champions is their ability to deal with surprises in a positive way, even as these could wreck their venture. A good illustration is Aerodium, one of the leading companies offering wind-tunnels in Europe. The company was established by an engineer, stuntman, and passionate traveller, Ivars Beitans, who heads the Latvian Bungee Jumping Association and could not resist flying in a wind tunnel, and by Ansis Egle, also a sports enthusiast with good experience in marketing and promotional activities.

The idea to launch Aerodium came initially from Beitans, who saw the problems less so on the market side (how to sell the flying experience?) but surprisingly on the supply side (how to get right equipment?). "When we entered the market at the end of 2004, the wind tunnel technology had not been well developed yet. The wind tunnel we bought simply did not work!" commented Beitans. "I took this very seriously and started with basic things: aerodynamics and construction, studying and analyzing the all possible technologies to come up with the solution to our wind tunnel." Eventually he came up with an invention superior to any existing wind tunnel technology. And the leading manufacturer of wind tunnels was soon merged with Aerodium.

Using resources you have, however limited

Though the majority of hidden champions leaders are nowadays much wealthier than the average company in their country, many of them had scarce resources at start-up. But they learned how to use their limited means to create more resources. Take Martins Saulesspurens, the Latvian founder of BLUE Microphones which attained the biggest market share in North America in high-end microphones. He used the means at his disposal (old microphones) to launch a new business.

Martins, fascinated by both music and technology, graduated from engineering and started to work for the Academy of Music of Latvia as a director of the sound recording studio. Jazz music was of particular interest to him, but the access to jazz records in the Soviet Union was very restricted. In the search for jazz recordings, Martins established pen- friend relationships with jazz enthusiasts in the U.K. and U.S. During one visit to the US, Martins met a college professor who was studying Latvian music and wanted to become closely connected with Latvians. Thus, he proposed that Martin send his son to study at his college without any tuition fee. However, Martins still needed to cover expenses for his son's studies. In 1988, Martins obtained a handful of worn out microphones from Soviet film studios. He decided to repair those microphones and try to sell them during his next first visit in the USA. He sold them immediately, earned expense money for his son and discovered a lucrative business. It turned out that an "old junk" Soviet studio microphone could be sold for nearly $6000 USD. Later in 1995, he presented his repaired microphones at one of the foremost US exhibitions dealing with sound and technology, which created important business contacts and generated his first sales. He set up a company and in 2010 BLUE Microphone earned $14 million.

Commitment to a world of possibilities and dreams

Leaders of hidden champions behave like the world is full of possibilities, and the best illustration in our studies was provided by Rok Uršič, an engineer by education, a physicist and artist by temperament and soul, and an entrepreneur by profession, who founded Instrumentation Technologies, a Slovenian company which is today a leading provider of instrumentation for research institutes with accelerators and hadrons. The biggest challenge that his company faced was to figure out how to synchronize both digital and analog measuring technology with software in one product. Rok Uršč framed it this way in a recent interview:

There is no fine line between the energy drawn to crazy ideas and entrepreneurial reality. Entrepreneurship is like an artistic activity. It is about creating an art work. Like the artist also we entrepreneurs struggle with moments of stuckness and relentlessness before we come to the moments of clarity.... In my work, there is co-existence between doing the right thing and reflecting and questioning the existing direction. In this work, one should sense subjective certainty into what the company is doing. Path to it does not exist in business reports and financial statements. As a leader you should feel the power exactly in this subjective uncertainty, by which you then empower the employees. It is difficult to articulate how one can find the subjective certainty. We don't have the right language to describe this phenomenon. At best the path to internal strength and empowerment could be described by the theory of a blind spot, which one needs to bring to awareness. When you succeed with bringing the blind spots into the awareness, this internal certainty can be their transferred outside to collective of employees, customers, and other shareholders.

Some hidden champions seem to know how to "bring the future to the present," as Otto Scharmer puts it, by seeing reality with fresh eyes, spotting emerging patterns that inform future possibilities, digging into inner sources of creativity and will, sustaining the anxiety before new visions and solutions crystallize, and then acting in an instant to capitalize on new opportunities.

Acts based on intelligent altruism

Hidden champions in many business affairs behave more altruistically than one would expect is rational. One may think that altruism is irrational; however maybe it is only a superior form of rationality based in reciprocity rather than self-interest. It seems it is more the latter as illustrated by the story of Igor Akrapovič and his company with the same name, which is a leading producer of titanium exhaust systems for racing bikes in the world.

In 1990s Igor Akrapovič was a passionate racer in super bikes, with national and international triumphs. However, during his racing days he was dissatisfied with the quality of exhaust systems, the most frequent reason for failure during races. In search for a better solution, Igor in his garage started trying out new designs of exhaust solutions made of titanium. Eventually, he came to a solution which satisfied him. He offered it for professional testing to a German racing team that was impressed by the product and immediately gave Igor long-term cooperation. After quitting racing, Igor kicked-off his own venture, Akrapovič which became the preferred producer of exhausting system for Honda, Yamaha, Ducatti, and many other racing teams. Despite early struggles with his company's bottom-line, he collaborated with these teams without charge. And while competitors were paying between 100K to 400K € to put their brand names on the teams' bikes, Igor was working with the teams to develop the exhaust systems of tomorrow. Nowadays, Akrapovič is paid well for design of exhaust systems for OEMs, and his exhaust systems are highly prized and priced in the world of super bikes.

Deliberate ignorance of existing knowledge

One of the most interesting practices observed in some, though not all, hidden champions is to apparently ignore existing knowledge and best practices in order to come up with novel solutions. Iztok Špan is CEO of Tajfun, a mid-size company with 15M € in revenues and 140 employees, that sells logging winches for foresting and firewood processors, where logistics are considered of utmost importance. In the search for novel technological solutions for complex logistics challenges, Iztok emphasized the role of ignorance of existing solutions:

Analyzing the existing technological and logistics solutions would frame our mind. It would constrain us. We would think only along corridors of the solutions. We are doing it the other way. First, we develop our own solution, a prototype, however we imagine it should be. Of course it fails, but then we analyze the failure to see what we don't understand. Only then we begin studying the exiting solutions to see what we are missing. First you need to act, try out things. Without acting you don't know what to analyze anyway.

Minimizing the affordable loss

The final element of the dominant logic of hidden champions is related to their long-term investment decisions. When considering the placement of resources, hidden champion leaders prefer to use "affordable loss" instead of "expected return" as one decision criteria. A good illustration of this is Pipistrel, which holds the global leadership in ultra-light aircraft: gliders with auxiliary motors and electric ultra-light planes.

Pipistrel can be viewed as the world's leader in introducing new categories of ultra-light planes. When business opportunities are small, Pipistrel prospers. When opportunities get bigger, larger firms enter the market and Pipistrel steps out. As Ivo Boscarol, the founder of the company puts it, "We have only two options. First, to develop a new product category and cash it out in next five years and then die; or to invest all the funds back to development of a new category of ultra-light plane, get approval for it by national aviation agencies, and live further. We decided for the latter. It's tough, yet exciting!" Congruent with that Boscarol has decided to invest minimum funds in production resources. After a new ultra-light plane is designed, Pipistrel produces only the first five prototypes, performs all the quality tests, designs the tools for mass production, specifies technological standards, and then outsources activities to local producers. "That way we don't need to invest into expensive CMC machines which would run only two weeks per year."

Could their dominant business inhibit the successful growth of hidden champions in the future?

Based on the analysis so far, we had to ask ourselves: are there limits to hidden champions' long-term success? Growth brings organizational complexity and constraint. Ownership and governance become complicated; more shareholders bring diverse perspectives on strategic issues; and competitive battles often become more severe because of the maturing of a market niche. A nice example of the upsides and downsides of growth is Optotek, a Slovene ophthalmic laser company set up by Boris Vedlin, Matjaž Zalar, and Majan Drašler, which launched an IPO on the Warsaw Stock Exchange in 2009 and was then acquired by Canon.

According to co-founder Vedlin, "After being acquired by Canon, most of my times go for planning and reporting on our financial performance. ... Japanese really know how to formalize a system and control the smallest detail... They work by manuals and pre-defined standards. ... No space for improvisation." He goes on, "Canon does not understand the laser technology. This is not passive technology as those in their cameras. Laser systems are alive, active systems. Besides, ophthalmic lasers are produced in small quantities, from 100 to 200," Another struggle Vedlin has is related to innovation and long-term perspective. "I know how to create and run a company that is constantly developing new products, technologies and conquers new markets! I can triple the revenues of the company in five years, but I cannot grow with 20 percent annual growth rate every year. In next five years I want to invest in ophthalmic lasers systems based on multiple wave lights and integrate our eye treatment lasers with eye diagnostics lasers technology."

The problem is that Canon requires Optotek to completely self-finance its operations with a right to get only short-term liquidity loans only from the internal Canon bank. What would Mr. Vedlin and Optotek need to do to increase their chances of success and future growth while still being part of Canon system? Taking a page from companies that have been acquired, one strategy would be for the acquiree to outline how new ophthalmic laser systems could address threats and opportunities in the market and boost the growth of parent-company Canon. In turn, acquired managers would also need to listen carefully to the parent company to understand its future technological investment plans and accommodate Optotek's vision of ophthalmic laser technology to them.

Once hidden champions are discovered and acquired, their managers have two options: either they master more "traditional" managerial outlooks and practices to conform to their parent company's culture or they gain the freedom and running room to continue to operate as semi-independent champions.

Some concluding remarks

The worlds of executive managers and leaders of hidden champions are about choice making. Hidden champions choose to operate like entrepreneurs where optimism, foresight, openness to possibilities, intelligent altruism, and so on are sources of competitive strength. These are not the competencies taught in most management and business schools, but we stress them in programs at IEDC and encourage participants to cultivate them in a career of life-long learning.

Of course, new situations, including acquisition, the maturation of markets, and growth all call for perhaps a more measured, traditional executive management model. In these instances, a blending of the business-making style of hidden champions and executive managers would most likely work best: seeing opportunities with constraints; using resources you have but acknowledging also resources you lack; acknowledging the worlds of possibility and reality; balancing intelligent altruism with calculative opportunism; blending innovative ignorance with knowledge; and minimizing the affordable loss while maximizing the expected returns. Thus, executive managers can learn a lot from leaders of hidden champion companies and vice versa.

Where can we find an illustration of a leader and organization that is good at both styles of business making—combining the hidden champion as well as the executive managerial style? Perhaps a good example is found in Danica Purg and IEDC that balances entrepreneurism with high quality management.

→ BUSINESS AS UNUSUAL: ARTS-BASED LEARNING AND PRACTICE

Ian Sutherland

On the day that you read this 130,000 new webpages will be launched, 290 billion emails and 27 million tweets will be sent, 360 million internet searches will be completed sifting through a trillion pages of content, 130 million people will be born (57 million will die), 73 species will go extinct, 54 new words will be added to the English language, and 1000 new businesses will begin. In fact, those numbers will have increased by the time you read this, and they will increase tomorrow, and the next day, and the next day.

The world of now is no longer the world of five minutes from now. We live in a post-modern, post-traditional, multi-everything (cultural, ethnic, religious, gender, etc.) world in which our perspectives and circumstances are constantly challenged and changed. Our senses, perceptions, and taken for granted modes of relating to the world—conventions, assumptions, ideologies—are increasingly inapt. How do we deal with this and in particular how do managers and organizational leaders operate amidst such change, complexity, and incongruity?

What we need are more sophisticated and sensitive ways to approach management and leadership education and practice which help people to recognize and navigate the complex human, social, sensory-emotional experiences of their daily work and life. This calls for an aesthetic approach—of skilled sensing, perceiving and acting—so that at each perspectival and circumstantial challenge they encounter, managers and leaders are capable of handling the complexity around them, making sense of it, and acting responsibly.

Traditional means of management and leadership education fail to prepare individuals for these complex dynamics. Even without reading the works of management gurus current and past, such as Henry Mintzberg and Peter Drucker, personal experiences of global economic crises, inequality, climate change, and so on tell us that "business as usual" is moving us down a darkening path. Yet the path need not be dark. To create, grasp, and realize a promising future, we can move from "business as usual" to "business as unusual."

Challenges and opportunities ahead require innovative approaches, new visions, and creative capacities. The realities of now and tomorrow call for management and leadership practices that issue from deep awareness of self and others furnished with inner will and aimed toward actions that are passionate, compassionate, and responsible. It is in the service of these goals that IEDC practices a business as unusual alchemy of melding management and leadership education with arts-based aesthetic experiences. In fact, this is exactly what attracted me to IEDC and led to my relocation from the Atlantic shores of my native Newfoundland and Labrador (Canada) to the Slovene shores of Lake Bled. This behooves a word of explanation.

Admittedly I have an "odd" background and professional pedigree. I was originally trained as a musician. For several years I worked exclusively within the arts–as a professional musician (pianist, organist, and choral conductor) and in management of arts organizations. This work–particularly seeing, feeling and being a part of the enriching, developmental and catalyzing power of music and the arts--drew me to the U.K. to pursue Ph.D. work in cultural sociology and philosophy. At this time I also became involved in researching leadership in the creative and cultural industries. Fast forward several years and I found myself invited to IEDC, ostensibly to consider a job here. Needless to say I was intrigued. When I arrived intrigue became inspiration. To my delight, here at the foot of the Julian Alps I found an institution whose vision, values, and activities so much matched my own. Here I found a management school dedicated to the enriching, developmental, and positive catalytic possibilities of the arts for individuals, organizations, and societies. It was not long before I felt compelled to join this history and contribute to its future.

From its inception IEDC incorporated cultural, artistic, aesthetic activities into its degrees and programs. In the beginning these events complimented professional workshops, seminars, and classes by enlivening participants' experiences with concerts, expositions and theatre outside the traditional classroom setting. These were never merely extra-curricular events. They were incorporated into the overall IEDC experience as means of inspiring students to grow capabilities in knowing oneself, in feeling how people are connected in expressive, emotional, and embodied ways, and in developing aesthetic awareness in perceiving, reflecting, and sensemaking.

When IEDC moved to the shores of Lake Bled, the commitment to art and aesthetics became not only a central philosophy but a very present physical manifestation. The current IEDC-Bled campus is a beautiful architectural venue incorporating the alpine lake surroundings in an art gallery approach. When students, staff, faculty, and visitors enter the school they enter art-filled spaces with paintings and sculptures. This approach comes from a deep-seated belief that when individuals and groups engage with the arts—visual, musical, literary, dramatic, etc.—they can be moved to hear, see, feel and most importantly act in more sensitive and positive ways. Over the years the school's artistic activities have expanded and today IEDC's students are directly engaged in and out of the classroom by expert arts faculty. Within our programs--from MBA to many tailor-made in company programs—participants learn about creativity, innovation, leadership, communication, and social, moral, and ethical issues through the arts.

Through this engagement we move well beyond business as usual education to help our students develop more sophisticated and sensitive ways of approaching the world that yield more aesthetic, passionate, and responsible management and leadership practices. Our integration of art-based methods is our way of developing the best, most reflective, most holistic leaders for the betterment of a global future.

Arts and Leadership in Practice

What does all this mean in practice? In rather large brush strokes, admittedly colored with a certain idealism, I have so far painted a wide philosophical canvas. What are the dynamics of IEDC's aesthetic philosophy towards business education? There are three central and overarching concepts which pedagogically inform our work in arts-based methods, all of which issue from IEDC's commitment to experiential, action-based learning. What we do is 1) create aesthetic workspaces for 2) self-development through aesthetic reflexivity which creates 3) memories with momentum.

In our teaching, we strive to create aesthetic workspaces by designing and crafting learning environments that capture the attention and imagination of participants and provide learning opportunities which engage them at expressive, emotional, and embodied levels. This sets the stage for meaningful self-work tailored towards helping participants to explore their own selves and to better understand who they are as individuals, managers and leaders. By making clear bridges between artistic activities and organizational life, we support them to examine their roles and practices and to reflect on how they relate to themselves, others, and the wider world.

What this develops is an aesthetic reflexivity—the feeling and knowing of self in divergent contexts—that helps participants to appropriate the aesthetics of experience, make deeper meaning of experience, and then more artfully understand the human dynamics encountered. It is through self-work that individuals learn to see themselves as both being and becoming a leader and to reflect on how they act in relation to the real, complicated, and sometimes messy social contexts of organizations.

Finally, these experiences, colored by unusual, multi-sensory, and emotionally- engaging events, create memorable memories of unique felt experience which remain active for participants well into the future. These are not just pleasant memories of music, theatre, film, or dance but active memories which students take into the world of work to form and evaluate their future business practice. They are memories that have future resonance, memories with momentum.

To Artful Managing and Leading

Working with this pedagogical foundation, we put the arts into action in three broad areas of management and leadership education. Think back to the beginning of this essay to thousands of new webpages launched, billions of emails issued, trillions of pages of web content scanned, and massive numbers of births, deaths, and extinctions daily, as well as untold possibilities on the horizon. It is in this context that we help program participants to manage and lead.

Increasingly managing and leading are about awareness of self and others amidst this complexity, being able to interpret it and organize it into understandable representations and communicate this meaningfully to others. In our arts-based classes we help participants
1) to embrace, manage, and communicate complexity;
2) to develop the creative leadership required to develop innovative solutions; and
3) to move beyond theory to actually experiencing and practicing the situational complexities of managing and leading people.

Artists and their products are highly adept at doing this. Artists embrace the complexity of experience in creative ways and develop innovative products with the power to move, inspire and compel people to action. Take, for example, Picasso's *Guernica*. This painting captures the violence and horror of the human experience of war, communicates this in a visceral, emotional way, and stimulates in us a revulsion of conflict. At IEDC, Professor Arnold Walravens introduces participants to the visual arts from a spectrum of historical periods to teach them about the various world perspectives depicted and to help them develop their own interpretive abilities. Arnold works with them to create parallels between their own perspectives and those employed by artists so that participants develop different ways of sensing, perceiving, interpreting, and communicating the world around us. This immersion in visual arts and in self raises questions and challenges participants about how to inspire others and motivate them to action.

While the products of artists point us towards new ways of approaching the management and leadership of complex experiences, actually engaging in the process of making art enlivens the creative and innovative capacities of all of us as human beings. Calls for more creative and caring modes of managing and leading come from many sources but taken together point to the need for a more creative response by organizations to the problems and opportunities that surround us. Contemporary and future organizations will remain sustainable only if they have the ability to anticipate and adapt to these circumstances; and they can only fully anticipate and adapt to them by knowing and questioning deeply the assumptions behind and creative potential emanating from their business models, and, where appropriate, developing more sustainable ones.

Faculty members such as myself work with students to develop deeper understandings of the creative processes employed by artists and how to manage and lead these processes. For example, students experience John Cage's "silent piece," 4 minutes and 33 seconds (*4'33"*) in which there are no pitches or rhythms written down by the composer. Rather, in *4'33"* Cage instructs the performer(s) to remain silent for a total of 4 minutes and 33 seconds. In this work Cage challenges the very assumption which underlined the Western world's music industry since its beginning–that music was intentionally made sound. In a way which predicted processes such as open innovation, Cage also shatters the traditional relationship between composer, performer, and audience: the basic assumption that an audience sits passively to receive a work of art no longer applies. Rather, the consumer is the active participant in the music making, constructing the piece themselves out of the environmental sounds of the space. Through such experiences, participants learn how to see through complex realities to the very core assumptions which lie behind products, services, and even industries.

In coming to understand the creative processes which lie behind such radically innovative works, IEDC participants develop aesthetically furnished understandings of how to embed creativity in their own organizations: how to manage and lead teams which are aware of an organization's basic assumptions, develop repertoires of creative options, and strategically choose and realize options with the highest potential.

The third broad area of arts-based activity at the IEDC focuses on leadership and management in action. Despite all our abstract theories, management and leadership are anything but abstract and theoretical, they are real and experiential. Throughout our programs participants engage in role playing activities, public speaking, presentations, and so on. Within their arts experiences there are two key courses which highlight the actual in practice complexities of managing and leading.

One deals with leaders on the big screen, the second on the podium. Professor Haris Pašović, an acclaimed film-director from Sarajevo, introduces participants to leadership through films. In works such as *Braveheart* (depicting the struggles of William Wallace and the First War of Scottish Independence) and *1492: The Conquest of Paradise* (showing the heroism and harms of Columbus' epic voyage), Haris develops deep conversations with participants about leadership in critical situations. Together they develop profound aesthetic understandings of leadership dilemmas, actions and outcomes by watching and discussing them unfold in dramatic form. In particular, Haris broadens the leadership perspective to understand the essential role of followership—that without followers, there are no leaders. All of this engages students around the ethics, morality, and overall purposes of leadership and management.

On the podium with Professor Peter Hanke, a Danish choral and operatic conductor, participants explore leadership from an embodied and highly interactive perspective. In the daily work environment, business professionals rarely get to experience their management and leadership actions in real time, less so with constructive feedback. With Peter Hanke students learn the basics of conducting and then step in front of a choir to conduct them through a piece of classical music. Students learn that leadership is not just about what you say or write, but that it is very much about what you do. They experience leadership as a holistic activity, that it is an embodied activity of gestures, facial expressions, and feeling the intangible connections between people working together to create something beautiful.

These examples are but a sample of the various arts-based activities that take place at IEDC. Through the aesthetic workspaces we create, our participants develop the aesthetic, reflexive skills of management and leadership which prepare them for the challenges of tomorrow. The core value of this activity is how arts-based education helps us and our participants re-envision and re-imagine what it means to manage and lead. These are innovative, business as unusual approaches, uniquely motivating and inspiring, which foster effective and lasting learning in the present and the future.

Ballet of the Boats on the Lake of Bled, composed by Vinko Globokar, 20th Anniversary of IEDC, 2006

Vinko Globokar, composer, 2006

Meeting with Stephen Covey in Ukraine, 2006

Meeting with Philip Kotler, 2006

Artists Eduard Čehovin and Haris Pašović, 2004

Prof. Bill Fischer at IEDC, 2008

Painted IEDC Garage - with Eduard Čehovin, 2004

Prof. Arnold Walravens and President of Riko Mr. Janez Škrabec, 2003

The authors of the book Leaders and Teams - The Winning Partnership, 2004

Mr. Hiroshi Nagata, Mitsui Europe, 2006

Dutch Royal Family visiting IEDC, 2007

Former President of Slovenia Mr. Janez Stanovnik receiving Doctor Honoris Causa title, 2008

Prof. Charles Handy at IEDC, 2005

Prof. Nancy Adler with Danica Purg and the MBA student Anabel Dolenc-Bueno, 2006

Prof. Emeritus Edgar Schein from MIT Sloan School of Management, 2007

IEDC participants in class

H.M. Queen Elisabeth at the IEDC Conference on Sustainable Development, 2008

Professors Henry Mintzberg, Danica Purg and Jonathan Gosling, 2007

Mr. Franjo Bobinac, president of Gorenje and member of Supervisory Board of IEDC, 2005

Mr. Riccardo Illy, chairman of Gruppo Illy and member of Supervisory Board at IEDC, 2004

Prof. Ichak Adizes, the guru on change management, 2011

Dr. Nadya Zhexembayeva, Coca-Cola Chair for Sustainable Development, 2011

The main actors of Bled - Kopaonik Forum, 2009

Prof. Danica Purg with Professors Pierre Casse and Paul Claudel

Prof. Philip Stiles, Judge Business School, University of Cambridge, in class

Prof. Hermann Simon receiving Doctor Honoris Causa title, 2009

Mr. Blaž Golob, Prof. Slavoj Žižek and Prof. Danica Purg, 2009

IEDC participants during their break

IEDC participants in the seminar room

Dr. Nadya Zhexembayeva receiving on behalf of IEDC the award from the Mayor of Bled Mr. Janez Fajfar, 2011

Dr. Zlatko Lagumdžija, president of SD party and former prime minister of BiH at IEDC, 2009

Mr. Sandi Češko, president of Studio Moderna and member of IEDC Supervisory Board, 2011

SLP for BAE Systems in Sarajevo, since 1996

Eureko Senior Leaders Programme in Sarajevo, since 2010

Prof. Salman Mufti, Queen's School of Business, Canada

Prof. Fraser Johnson, Richard Ivey School of Business, Canada

President of Slovenia Dr. Danilo Türk at the UN Global Compact Slovenia event, 2011

Prof. Danica Purg, receiving the award "Dean of the Year 2010" by the Academy of International Business (AIB), 2010

Academic Director Prof. Nenad Filipović in class

Prof. Stephane Garelli lecturing at IEDC, 2010

Prof. Danica Purg with Mrs. Doris Drucker in the USA, 2009

Mr. Michael Slobodin, vice president TNK-BP Russia, talking at ELC conference 2011

Bill Clinton addressing the participants of the conference of Clinton initiative, 2011

CEEMAN Board meeting in Georgia, 2011

Dr. Ian Sutherland, Director of PhD studies in class

IEDC staff cheering the IEDC rowing team, 2011

International Management Teachers Academy (IMTA)

IEDC-Bled School of Management – the main building

LESSONS FROM IEDC'S FIRST 25 YEARS

Philip H. Mirvis

In his study of *Leading Minds*, psychologist Howard Gardner stresses the importance of story-telling by leaders. "The story is a basic human cognitive form; the artful creation and articulation of stories constitutes a fundamental part of the leader's vocation. Stories speak to both parts of the human mind—its reason and emotion." He goes on, "I deliberately use the terms *story* and *narrative* rather than *message* or *theme*. In speaking of stories, I want to call attention to the fact that leaders present a dynamic perspective to their followers: not just a headline or snapshot, but a drama that unfolds over time in which they—the leaders and followers—are the principal characters or heroes." That has been the thrust of story-telling here about IEDC's first 25 years of history.

Many management and business books contain bullet-point lists of practical lessons and how to apply them. This IEDC learning history has also offered lessons for pragmatic readers, but they have not been bullet-pointed or enumerated. Hopefully they have nonetheless emerged—and different ones for different readers—from the narrative. Joe Pons, the marketing matador and proponent of teaching as a performance art, is of the same mind about leadership lists. He tells his students: "Management is about action, not laws like in physics. If I gave my students, say, the

40 laws of management, they would tune out by law #2." He adds, "You cannot photocopy management problems"—there are too many nuances that must be considered.

In this spirit, consider a few personal reflections and questions raised from experiencing IEDC and its people, history, and environs.

On People and Culture

You have read what René Magdalenić and Jim Ellert, two visiting professors, had to say about their first encounters with Slovenian and Balkan managers in the late 1980s—managers were not equipped for the pace and temper of a Western-style development program. Sensitive to stereotyping, René notes however that this has "nothing to do with their IQ or personal background; just two different worlds." He goes on to explain that the student population in those years was typically age 50 and older and came of age in the "old socialist system." Other Westerners coming into Slovenia and CEE countries were more ethnocentric in their outlooks and consequently came across as condescending.

The Russian sociologist Aleksandr Zinovyev coined the term "Homo Sovieticus" to describe the impact of seven decades of totalitarianism on the populace in his home country oft expressed in this Soviet-era joke: "they pretend to pay us and we pretend to work." While the former Yugoslavia was outside of the Soviet orbit, and based its economic system on worker "self-management," the business leaders interviewed in this study also acknowledged that some of their managers lacked initiative in this period and were not up to demands of operating in a faster, more market-oriented framework.

By contrast, Professor Krzysztof Obłoj from Poland sees the students and managers in a far different light today. On the diversity of its student body, he says, "There can be 18 different nationalities in a room, different cultures, styles, orientations. That is unusual in CEE business schools." He also finds CEE students to be "natural" entrepreneurs: "Students and managers from this region are always prepared to 'break the rules' or at least 'bend the rules.'" From decades of operating in a state- run system, "they know how to 'beat the system.'"

The students also think differently about business and the market. "Take western students: you put 8 balls in a glass, 7 black ones and 1 red one, and the westerners will bet that you will pick a black ball. They calibrate the odds. CEE students are more comfortable taking risks. They'll bet the red one." His challenge has been to make them more professional in thinking about innovating in the market and then to execute once they have a winning idea.

IEDC students appreciated diversity among fellow participants. Maja Ibrišimović, an MBA grad, recalls an amusing dialogue in her finance class about how to manage "receivables." A German student remarked that this was "no problem because my customers pay on time." A Bosnian countered that it was "a big problem" because most of her customers could not pay the bills, so that her company would have to arrange a loan to manage cash flow. A Russian student said that receivables were not a problem in his company. Why not? He replied, "I know a guy that can collect them."

There are, of course, many factors at work in the transformation of a people and cultures. In this region of the world, the shock of an economic makeover, wholesale changes in the political system, as well as globalized media and internet access and the emergence of a new generation into higher education and positions of power, all factor in. What is notable, however, is that even among this new generation of business leaders and MBAs in Slovenia and CEE countries, there remain strong sentiments in favor of traditional brotherhood and solidarity.

Based on IEDC's experiences, are there parallels in early encounters with and the subsequent development of business outlooks and culture in China? What is similar and different in the cases of India, Southeast Asia, South Africa, and Brazil?

On Doing Business

In *The Future of Industrial Man*, published in 1942, Peter Drucker claims that "the business corporation—or indeed any organization—is as much a social organization, a community and society, as it is an economic organ." He shared a draft of this manuscript with a friend, the economic historian Karl Polanyi, who resonated with the ideas and advanced the thesis further in his own volume, *The Great Transformation*, by claiming that reciprocity, rather than economic rationality, should guide the integration of business and society. To Drucker this meant that considerations of community and human relations should stand alongside economics and market forces in the practice of management.

In the U.S. and later the U.K. and Western Europe, these ideas have been supplanted by "agency theory," which contends, among other things, that managers' interests and incentives must be aligned wholly with those of financial shareholders and that executives must be monitored and controlled to prevent any opportunism that takes monies away from shareholders. This theory was the intellectual fuel behind the shareholder rights movement that began in the 1980s that has led to higher returns and bigger executive salaries and bonuses; but it also led to widespread and repeated waves of corporate restructuring, downsizing, hostile takeovers, cheap labor outsourcing, and the like. Managers' fixations on quarterly returns and short-term profit taking seem to be its enduring legacy.

Will this logic also take over in CEE business? Pay careful attention to the business leaders who contributed their stories to this learning history, including company presidents Janez Škrabec, of Riko, Franjo Bobinac, of Gorenje, Tatjana Fink, of Trimo, Riccardo Illy, of Group Illy, and Sandi Češko, of Studio Moderna: each of them to varying degrees has led their companies through painful retrenchment, modernized their workforces, plants, and product lines, and yet in doing so retained a sense of camaraderie and deepened their connections to the local communities, the region, and even the world.

Where does IEDC come out in relation to these two competing models of management responsibilities? At a recent meeting, Danica challenged her fellow Business School deans thusly: "Do we merely continue to promote money as the only meaningful outcome of executive education or is it finally the time to begin providing new and meaningful teaching frameworks, frameworks appropriate to reflection, honesty, and intellectual rigor that will be needed by our students and political and business leaders?"

As you reflect on this learning history, ask yourself as appropriate: Which model is operating in my business or my business school?

On Teaching and Learning

A thoughtful critic of management education, Professor Henry Mintzberg, of McGill University in Montreal, Canada, has this to say: "Many management programs promise "boot camp": Be prepared to work hard, they warn—this is no country club. Managers certainly don't need a country club atmosphere for their development, but neither do they need boot camp....Boot camps train soldiers to march and obey, not to stop and think. Managers today desperately need to stop and think. They need to step back from the action and reflect thoughtfully on the experience they live all too pervasively."

In his address at IEDC's 10th anniversary, Drucker spoke of the importance of reflection. He reminded the audience of the Socratic dictum to "know thyself," which he translated into a "mirror test" for managers. "Every morning when you look in the mirror, when you shave yourself or put on your lipstick: is the person you see in the mirror the person you want to see?" From the get-go, IEDC made self- reflection a core part of its identity and curriculum.

Another implication of the boot camp metaphor of management education is that learning comes from "breaking down" the student—through stressful work, and some humiliation, ostensibly in service of unlearning bad habits or attitudes and developing better ones. You have read here references by IEDC students to the MBA "jungle" and to shedding blood in their coursework. Colorful metaphors, but the prevailing ethos at IEDC has been instead on "building up" students, playing to strengths, and boosting their self-confidence.

Enzo Smrekar, a graduate of the President's MBA in 2007, very much "liked the respect" shown to IEDC students by the faculty. "They treat you like you are at the same level," he reports. "The professors are positive. They encourage you. Say 'you can do it.'" At other schools, he notes, "they don't do this." Enzo works today as an executive coach, inspiring his own charges.

Are these just fluffy self-help nostrums? Hardly. Drucker's dual emphasis on "self-knowledge" and "building on strengths" anticipated what has since become a cross- cultural movement in personal and organization development. Nadya talked about this in terms of appreciative inquiry. It is also represented in concepts like "learned optimism," "psychological hardiness," and "emotional resilience" that are making their way into management practice and in scholarly study at, for example, the Center for the Study of Positive Organizational Scholarship at the University of Michigan's Business School.

Does this have practical relevance to competitive students and businesses? Listen to MBA Ivana Jovović on her takeaways: "It's all about winning. That's right, winning. This is what we have learned here. But I'm not talking about the most points or market share. I'm talking about winning in a contest with your own potential....about never measuring your success based on the success of others-- because you just might set the bar too low."

How are the students in your school led—broken down or built up? How about employees in your organization?

On Art and Leadership

Danica claims she was inspired and got the confirmation of her efforts to promote arts and leadership from her visit to Peter Drucker's home in Claremont in 1995. In an article on this topic she writes, "It is well known that Peter Drucker admired Japanese art and that he made a great collection of it. He called his first exposure to Japanese art 'a pure accident, pure mistake'....He writes how on a sunny Saturday in the summer of 1934 he stopped on the way home from work to see what he thought would be the summer showing of painting by the Royal Academy members in London's Burlington Arcade. Instead, he found himself in an exhibition of Japanese paintings. He felt being pulled in and moved by this exotic, unfamiliar art...."

In this mythic story, recounted regularly by Danica to IEDC students, and also to journalists and educators, Drucker's genuine experience of enlightenment informed her own: "Peter Drucker convinced me that art can help a person to learn more about her or himself and helps you to become a better leader and manager," she says. Since that first inspiration, Danica and colleagues have developed a full portfolio of seminars and programs on arts and leadership. "From orchestras we can learn a lot about leading in difficult times, whereas jazz can inspire us to lead in good times because it allows more improvisation." She goes on, "An analysis of how artists are trained and how they work can produce important insights into what is needed to perform and what it means to lead and manage."

All of this is wrapped by IEDC into a value proposition for managers and students. Danica writes, "Our school is devoted to enhancing creativity. We define it as the ability to transcend traditional ideas, rules, patterns, and relationships and create meaningful new ideas, forms, methods, and interpretations. It is characterized by a sophisticated bending of conventions and an ability to produce something new through imaginative skills. Sociological and psychological studies show that creativity happens in the dynamic systems of organizations. It requires critical reflexivity—a deep awareness of yourself and the world around you. It is also about openness to ideas, contradictions and challenges...."

The learning history has illustrated aspects of the arts and leadership pedagogy at IEDC and how Ricardo Illy makes it central to the crafting and sale of coffee, chocolates, tea, fruit jams, and now wine in over 140 countries around the world. Considering the research imperative in the learning history, however, please note that while Drucker was himself a devotee of art, he never advocated that it be part of the education of the manager nor did he write explicitly about its connection to the practice of management although he mentioned the metaphor of jazz and the classical orchestra in one of his books in the 1950s.

That said, Danica made very practical use of Drucker's inspiration in developing and promoting the arts and leadership program at IEDC. And his inspiration was passed on to IEDC alumnae. Listen to how this MBA expressed this in a graduation speech by reminding classmates: "Peter Drucker and his love for Japanese art and his wife will chase us all the way to our sweetest dreams."

Consider, too, in your sweetest dreams what the practical relevance of connecting arts and leadership might mean for your school, your business, or yourself. Based on his experiences in bringing such dreams to life, Miha Pogačnik reflects, "I believe the arts will take on a very different role in future architecture of human society. This could be the cutting edge of innovation."

On "Next Steps" for IEDC

IEDC has already taken a global leadership role in arts and leadership. Given that "stretch" has been its animating motivation, where should it next reach in this direction? One step forward in arts and leadership would be to host international academic and executive conferences on this subject to cement its reputation and open the market for further business involvement. It could also make its contributions to art and leadership more broadly accessible by, for example, making its experiential teaching exercises available via streaming video or by taking its show "on the road" to other management development centers, business schools, or businesses. Stretching its own organizational boundaries, it might liaise with design schools in the region or globally to extend its footprint and enhance its practical pedagogy.

On the CSR and sustainability front, the school today offers its growing expertise to business executives, government officials, and students in business and public management. There is today also growing interest in "social innovation" which combines knowledge and resources from business, government, *and* civil society to create innovations that address social and environmental challenges. Dr. Maximilian Martin, Faculty in Residence, Ashoka University, USA, and founder of Impact Economy, Switzerland, excited many in the audience at IEDC's conference with the Clinton Global Initiative when he talked about an emerging category of business and societal leaders who are called "social entrepreneurs."

What characterizes a social entrepreneur? Martin enumerated the characteristics: mission driven, opportunity oriented, innovative, resourceful, and accountable. While the young people in attendance nodded in agreement, perhaps finding "who I am" in this listing, it was also apparent that they were in search of resources to develop their talents in this arena and for validation of this as a career calling.

Danica spoke to these aspirations when she said at conference, "At IEDC, we have made the commitment to find more space for social entrepreneurship in our programs in the future, to devote one of our future conferences to best practices in social entrepreneurship, to develop consulting projects in the field of social entrepreneurship by our participants, and to have at least one social entrepreneur in our longer courses, based on a scholarship initiative." That is a modest next step. Looked onward, executive development centers have not yet envisioned how to define or reach a market of social entrepreneurs, as students or practitioners, nor formulated a coherent and innovative curriculum for them, nor developed faculty members skilled in this subject matter and practice. IEDC could take a leadership role in this space by not only "taking the best" of what becomes available but also by co-creating in partnership with, say, citizen-sector organization Ashoka or other "nontraditional" players, a world-class pedagogy and developmental programs on social entrepreneurship.

Over the past twenty-five years, IEDC has stretched and grown though its networks, many created by Danica, and is today a lead player in CEEMAN, ELC, AACORN, PRME, and a number of other international associations. Still, IEDC does not possess the wealth, faculty resources, or international reputation of the biggest and best management education schools in Western Europe or the U.S. nor does it have the influence of the London, Harvard, or other leading Business Schools that are connected to large and prestigious universities. How can IEDC compete with them in the global marketplace?

A tour around the world shows that the Gibbs Business School, in Johannesburg, South Africa, Babson College, in the U.S., with its top-rated program for business entrepreneurs, Ipade Business School in Mexico City and Insper-Ibmec São Paulo each qualify as the "best small business school" in their respective regions. Any or all of these schools are possible partners in globalizing IEDC's students and management development programs and in opening Slovenia's border to new visitors and business opportunities.

Reinventing Executive Development

Finally, consider how the vision and the voices of IEDC-Bled School of Management point the way to reinventing business education and leadership development in a world that badly needs it. Danica was a contributor to the first Global Roundtable for Advanced Management Education Reform held in the U.S. in 2009 and has been a visible advocate in many forums for making ethics, sustainability, and global corporate citizenship central to the curriculum and culture of management schools. IEDC has, to this point, led by example. It is primed for more vocal leadership and advocacy by its local and extended faculty, its students and alumni, its business partners, and its Supervisory and Academic Advisory bodies in these regards.

From the start, IEDC embodied Peter Drucker's vision of management as a "liberal art" and stretched its curriculum to incorporate foundational material on ethics and aesthetics, as well as vivid learning experiences that stimulate reflections on history, philosophy, the natural environment, the political-economy, and especially one's self. By doing so, IEDC is today preparing a next-generation to operate on a global scale not simply as business leaders, but also as humanists, activists, and statesmen and women. Shouldn't other business and management schools also aspire to this and make the necessary adaptations?

This 25 year history has depicted IEDC metaphorically as a bumblebee that didn't know it couldn't fly and soared to unimagined heights. Its progression—from taking the best from the west, to sharing with and learning from peers, then to innovating in new directions and in novel ways—has been its unique trajectory and should not be construed as *the* "model" for other schools, even those just beginning to take flight in developing economies and to grapple with the contradictions between market capitalism and responsible leadership.

However, there are some takeaways for management school deans and educators from IEDC's history. Many of its innovations in program content, development, design, and delivery are relevant and could prove inspirational to faculties, students, and businesses in both the developing and developed worlds. When that is the case, take a page from the example from Sandi Češko of Studio Moderna and "minnovate" with them. But pay attention, especially, to the larger story here: the alchemy of combining IEDC's vision and mission, foresight and flexibility, and its courage to take risks with its commitment to be an agent of change. This story yields lessons on academic leadership.

→ NOTES AND REFERENCES BY CHAPTER AND SECTION

Introduction

Peter Drucker quotes from "Manage Yourself and Then Your Company: Set an Example." International Executive Development Center. Brdo, Slovenia. 1997.

Francis Fukuyama, *The End of History and the Last Man* (New York: Free Press, 1992); on alternative artist's vision, see Bruce Sterling, "1989: The End of History or the Beginning of the Future?" *Wired*, November 4, 2009.

Background in Peter Drucker, *Adventures of a Bystander* (New York: John Wiley & Sons, 1994).

Part I Synopsis: 25 Years of Making History
Peter Hain quote on IEDC as the best little business school in Europe from interview by Andrew Grice, *The Independent*, April 23, 2002.

Best from the West
Danica Purg quote on early days of school from interview by Penny Haw, "Management: Learning the Art of Leadership," *Business Day,* June 6, 2011.

Leading through Innovation
On new economies, see Nancy J. Adler, Leading Beautifully: The Creative Economy and Beyond, *Journal of Management Inquiry, 20,* 3, 2011, 208–221; B. Joseph Pine II and James H. Gilmore, *The Experience Economy* (Boston: Harvard Business School Press, 1999).

Part II Synopsis: Founder and Faculty Reflections
On learning histories, see Art Kleiner and George Roth, "How to Make

tion threaten the quality of what we teach our future business leaders." *European Business Forum*, Autumn, 2007.

Janez Škrabec, Quest of Discovery

Riko website at http://www.rikogroup.com/en/; also see Janez Škrabec "Innovative for 130 Years," *The Future Book*, Third Millennium Knowledge BV, The Netherlands and TMK Lab d.o.o., Slovenia, 2010.

2. Take the Best from the West—and Leave the Rest

Derek Abell, "Management Education in Emerging Markets: What is the Same, What is Different?" Management Education for the Realities of Emerging Markets, Proceedings of the 16th CEEMAN Annual Conference, Tirana, Albania, September 25-27, 2008.

Business Case Teaching

On case teaching see Louis B. Barnes, C. Roland Christensen, and Abby Hansen, Teaching and the Case Method, 3rd Ed. (Boston: Harvard Business School Press, 1994).

Student Teams and Projects

Nenad Filipović, "Teaching General Management," *Business Leadership Review,* 7, 4, 2010.

Tom Piper quoted in "Case Method in Practice." C. Roland Christensen Center for Teaching and Learning, Harvard Business School website.

Institutional Isomorphism?

Karl Polanyi, *The Great Transformation: The Political and Economic Origins of Our Time (Boston: Beacon Press, 1994).*

Nina Bandelj, "Market Transition 'One MBA at a Time:' Institutionalization of Management Education in Central and Eastern Europe." Research Network 1989, WP 2008/5.

They Don't Understand Us!

Thomas J. Peters, "The American Way of Managing--A Model for the Whole World?" International Executive Development Center. Brdo, Slovenia. 1991; also see Thomas J. Peters and Robert H. Waterman, Jr. *In Search of Excellence* (New York: Harper & Row, 1982).

Nancy G. McNulty with Alexander Katkov, Management Education in Eastern Europe: 'fore and after." *Academy of Management Executive*, 6, 4, 1992: 78-87

Networking in CEE

For more background, also see "Management Education in Transition: Interview with Andrzej Koźmiński" *CEEMAN News*, 42, Winter, 2006.

Enter George Soros

Karl Popper, *The Open Society and Its Enemies* (London: Routledge, 1945).

Soros quoted in "Rich man, wise man..." *The Observer*, March, 10, 2002

Forming CEEMAN

Select quotes from 10th Anniversary video, CEEMAN

"Shock Therapy" for the Yugoslav Economy

On Sachs and shock therapy, see Peter Passell, "Dr. Jeffrey Sachs, Shock Therapist," *New York Times Magazine*, June 27, 1993; on critiques see Naomi Klein, *The Shock Doctrine: The Rise of Disaster Capitalism* (New York, Picador, 2007); quote from Ellerman reported in "The long, strange career of Jeffrey Sachs." Left Business Observer, #111, August, 2005.

Yugoslav President Borisav Jović from British Broadcasting Service, Borisav Jović Tells SFRY Assembly Situation Has Dramatically Deteriorated, 27 April 1991.

Tatjana Fink, Women Leading
Tatjana Fink in "TrimTeam" 10 December, 2010 and Trimo www.trimo.eu.

Daniel Goleman, *Emotional intelligence* (New York: Bantam, 1995).

3. 10 Day War

For background on 10 day war, see Laura Silber and Allan Little, *The Death of* Yugoslavia (London: Penguin, 1995).

The Breakup of Yugoslavia
Janez Drnovšek, "Riding the Tiger: The Dissolution of Yugoslavia," *World Policy Journal, Spring, 2000.*

War in the Balkans
On the yogurt revolution, see Sabrina Petra Ramet and Vjeran Pavlaković (ed). *Serbia Since 1989: Politics and Society Under Milošević and After* (Seattle, WA: University of Washington Press, 2005); Milošević quoted in Heike Krieger (ed), *The Kosovo Conflict and International Law: An Analytical Documentation 1974-1999* (Cambridge: Cambridge University Press, 2001

On Tragedy and Leadership
Jonathan Gosling and Henry Mintzberg, "5 Minds of a Manager" *Harvard Business Review November, 2003.*

Assembling a Seminar in Sarajevo
Zlatko wounding "9 Slain, 100 Wounded in Serb Attack on Sarajevo," Manila Standard, May 24, 1993. Posted on May 1, 2011 by Bosnian Genocide.

On the Sarajevo workshop, Jonathan Gosling and Danica Purg, "How to be Sanguine in Sarajevo: Leadership as Transformation or Tragedy?" B.A.W.B. Interactive Working Paper Series, 1, 3, Article 6, 2007.

Susan Sontag "Waiting for Godot in Sarajevo," *Performing Arts Journal*, 16, 2, 1994, 87-106.

A Modern Monastery
George Bickerstaffe, "Thoroughly Modern Monasteries, *Financial Times*, January 10, 2005.

Franjo Bobinac, Innovation and Design
Background on Gorenje at http://www.gorenje.com/; also see Lynn A. Isabella, Gerry Yemen, Hatem Hatem, and Nenad Filipović, "Gorenje D.D.: Evolution or Revolution," University of Virginia, Darden Business Publishing, 2006.

Gorenje Ora-Ito Collection," *de zeen magazine*, May 13, 2007.

4. Program Innovations

Beth Collins, "World's most beautiful lakes," CNN Travel, August 12, 2010.

Milenko Gudić quoted in Kester Eddy, "Common Ground across Continents," Financial Times, October 15, 2006, 16-18.

IMTA-International Management Teaching Academy
Randy Kudar "Developing Teaching Skills," New Challenges of Faculty Development, In Proceedings of the Deans and Directors Meeting, 13th CEEMAN Annual Conference, Kiev, Ukraine, September 22, 2005.

Research: Rigor or Relevance?
Thomas G. Cummings, "Presidential Address: Quest for an Engaged Academy," Academy of Management Annual Meeting, Atlanta, GA, August 2006; for more see Rajesh Khurana, *From Higher Aims to Hired Hands* (Princeton, NJ: Princeton University Press, 2007).

"IMTA touches peoples' lives." Milenko Gudić Interview with IMTA faculty-- Krzysztof Obłoj, JB Kassarjian, Joe Pons, Arshad Ahmad, and Jim Ellert. *CEEMAN News*, 56, Summer, 2010.

Leadership and the Arts
Miha Pogačnik quotes from website http://www.mihavision.com/

Riccardo Illy, Business Artist in Trieste
Illy website at http://www.illy.com/wps/wcm/connect/us/illy/ Francesco Illy and Riccardo Illy, *Dal Caffe all'Espresso* (Milan: A. Mondadori, 1994).

Leading through Authenticity
Nancy J. Adler, Leading Beautifully: The Creative Economy and Beyond, *Journal of Management Inquiry, 20, 3, 208*–221.

5. Making a Better World

Milan Kučan, "Challenges for the Future," in "Competitiveness of Companies in Central and Eastern Europe." International Executive Development Center. Bled, Slovenia. 2001; Samuel P. Huntington. *The*

Clash of Civilizations and the Remaking of World Order (New York: Simon & Schuster, 1996).

Engaging with Society

Danica Purg, Jonathan Gosling and Pierre Casse in "Creating an Agenda for European Leadership," The European Leadership Centre, Conference Proceedings, Bled, Slovenia, June 10-11, 2003.

Bringing Creativity into Business Education

Danica Purg on crossroads in "Looking Ahead," New Global Performance Challenges and Implications for Management Development", Proceedings of the 18th CEEMAN Annual Conference, Caserta/Naples, Italy, September 23-25, 2010.

Bringing Creativity into Business

On performativity, see Philip H. Mirvis, Karen Ayas, and George Roth, *To the Desert and Back: The Story of One of the Most Dramatic Business Transformations on Record* (San Francisco: Jossey-Bass, 2003); also Philip H. Mirvis and Tex Gunning, Creating a community of leaders. *Organizational Dynamics*, 35, 1, 2006, 69-82.

Expanding IEDC's Mission and Reach

Leadership for a Better World. International Executive Development Center. 20th anniversary, Bled, Slovenia. 2006.

Challenge:Future

Christopher Laszlo and Nadya Zhexembayeva, *Embedded Sustainability: The Next Big* Competitive Advantage (Palo Alto, CA: Stanford Business Books, 2011).

Nmetro story at http://www.challengefuture.org/news/310

Sandi Češko, Commercial and Social Entrepreneur

Sandi Češko interview in "Entrepreneurship in Your DNA." *The Future Book*, Third Millennium Knowledge BV, The Netherlands and TMK Lab d.o.o., Slovenia, 2010. Dan Isenberg, "Entrepreneurs: Stop Innovating, Start Minnovating" HBR Blog Network, November 19, 2009.

IEDC and the Clinton Global Initiative

Violeta Bulc at http://www.violeta.si/

On the new science, see Margaret J. Wheatley, *Leadership and the New Science: Learning about Organization from an Orderly Universe* (San Francisco: Berrett- Koehler, 1993).

On presence, see Peter M. Senge, C. Otto Scharmer, Joseph Jaworski and Betty Sue Flowers, *Presence: An Exploration of Profound Change in People, Organizations, and Society* (New York: Currency, 2004).

Social Entrepreneur

Gazmend Haxhia in "A Portrait Gallery of Albanian Entrepreneurs: Riding on the Waves of Change." Southeast Europe Business Guides, 2009/2010; http://www.universitetipolis.org/

Postscript

Adizes background at http://www.adizes.com/; Ichak Adizes, *Managing Corporate Lifecycles: How and Why Corporations Grow and Die and What to Do About It?* (Englewood Cliffs, NJ: Prentice-Hall, 1998).

Strategy as Stretch

Mariola Ciszewska-Mlinarič, "Strategy as a fit or stretch? Implications for International Entrepreneurship, paper delivered at 31st International Conference on Entrepreneurship and Innovation, Maribor, Slovenia, April 20-21, 2011; also see Gary Hamel and C.K. Prahalad,

Competing for the Future, Boston: Harvard Business Press, 1984 and James Collins and Jerry Porras, "Building Your Company's Vision," *Harvard Business Review,* 74, 5, 1996: 65–77.

What's Next
Peter Drucker, "The Discipline of Innovation, *Harvard Business Review*, November- December, 1988.

Essay on Networking

Herminia Ibarra and Mark Hunter, "How Leaders Create and Use Networks," *Harvard Business Review, 85, 1, 2007, 40-47, 124.*

Nina Bandelj and Danica Purg, "Networks as Resources, Organizational Logic, and Change Mechanism: The Case of Private Business Schools in Post-Socialism, *Sociological Forum*, *21*, 4, 2006, 587-622.

Essay on IEDC Lessons

On doing business
Peter Drucker, *The Future of Industrial Man,* 2nd Ed. (Rutgers, NJ: Transaction, 1995). On agency theory, see Sumatra Ghoshal, "Bad management theories are destroying good management practices." *Academy of Management Learning & Education*, *4*, 1, 2005: 75-91.

On teaching and learning
Henry Mintzberg, *Managers Not MBAs: A Hard Look at the Soft Practice of Managing and Management Development* (San Francisco: Berrett-Koehler, 2004).

SUPERVISORY BOARD MEMBERS OF IEDC-BLED SCHOOL OF MANAGEMENT

President: *Dr. Erhard Busek,* Chairman of Institute for the Danube Region and Central Europe, Austria

Vice President: *Prof. Derek F. Abell,* Professor Emeritus, ESMT - European School of Management and Technology, Germany

- *Mr. Franjo Bobinac,* Chairman of the Management Board, Gorenje, Slovenia
- *Mr. Sandi Češko,* President of the Board, Studio Moderna Group, Slovenia
- *Ms. Tatjana Fink,* General Manager, Trimo, Slovenia
- *Mr. Riccardo Illy,* Chairman, Gruppo Illy, Italy
- *Mr. Zoran Janko,* Chief Executive Officer, Mobitel, Slovenia
- *Dr. Peter Kraljič,* Director Emeritus, McKinsey & Co., Germany
- *Ms. Cvetka Selšek,* President of the Management Board, SKB Banka, Slovenia
- *Mr. Klemen Šešok,* Managing Director, Taxgroup, Slovenia
- *Dr. Gregor Veselko, President of the Management Board, Luka Koper, Slovenia*

→ OWNERS OF IEDC-BLED SCHOOL OF MANAGEMENT

STUDIO MODERNA D.O.O.
MOBITEL D.D.
RIKO INVEST D.O.O.
TAXGROUP D.O.O.
LUKA KOPER D.D.
KRKA D.D.
BTC D.D.
LEK D.D.
TELEKOM SLOVENIJE D.D.
PETROL D.D.
GORENJE D.D.
OBČINA BLED
NOVA KBM D.D.
PIVOVARNA LAŠKO D.D.
PROBANKA D.D.
ISTRABENZ D.D.
TRIMO D.D.
SALONIT ANHOVO D.D.
AERODROM LJUBLJANA D.D.
MERKUR D.D.
ZAVAROVALNICA TRIGLAV D.D.
PERUTNINA PTUJ D.D.
ENERGOPLAN D.D.
KS NALOŽBE D.D.
STEKLARNA HRASTNIK D.D.
DELOITTE D.O.O.
COMTRADE D.O.O.
INTEREUROPA D.D.
SKB BANKA D.D.
HIDRIA D.D.

Publisher:
IEDC-Bled School of Management

Editors:
Danica Purg, Arnold Walravens,
Barbara Vilfan

Design:
Eduard Čehovin

DTP:
Primož Urgl

Year:
2011

Circulation:
1,500 copies

Printed by **Ednas Print d.o.o.**